S.99

WITH MAGIC I

sf

Also available in this series:

WITH MAGIC IN MY EYES

A CORNISH CHRONICLE

by

Erma Harvey James

"When I came back from Lyonesse
With magic in my eyes"
Thomas Hardy

ISIS
LARGE PRINT
Oxford and Orlando

First published in Great Britain 1998
by Tabb House

Published in Large Print 1999 by ISIS Publishing Ltd,
7 Centremead, Osney Mead, Oxford OX2 0ES, and
ISIS Publishing, PO Box 195758,
Winter Springs, Florida 32719-5758, USA
by arrangement with Tabb House Publishers

British Library Cataloguing in Publication Data
James, Erma Harvey
    With magic in my eyes. – Large print ed.
    1. James, Erma Harvey – Childhood and youth 2. Large type
    books 3. Cornwall (England) – Social life and customs – 20th
    century
    I. Title
    942.3'7'082'092

ISBN 0-7531-5715-2 (hb)
ISBN 0-7531-5736-5 (pb)

Printed and bound by Antony Rowe, Chippenham and Reading

ACKNOWLEDGEMENTS

These Acknowledgements were to have been published above Dion Byngham's signature, having been completed less than a month before his death in 1990. They appear as they stood, with the publisher's regret that neither the author nor editor was able to see the book in print and that the exigencies of publishing have led to considerable delay in the production of the book.

My sincere appreciation and thanks were due to Olive and the late George Ordish, to Mary Spencer Watson, to Rosemary and Ida Pollock, to Dr Susan Compton, to Mr Richard Ings and Mr Lawrence Sail of South West Arts, to Ian and Jane, Denis Lowson and Maja, to Dr Edwin Miller, Mr Ernest Cooper, Caroline White, Joe Potts, and to Kyle Fulton for special typing help and, last but not least, to our daughter Julia Erma Dione, for their constant help and encouragement to me in seeing Erma's book home and dry. Thanks were also due to the late Rosalind Wade, OBE. Towards all good friends of Erma and myself who have supported me with their kindness and sympathy I feel deep gratitude. To them and to Julia, besides myself, this book was dedicated by Erma.

FOREWORD

Erma Harvey James wrote *With Magic in My Eyes* during the last two years of her life, leaving one half chapter and the Postscript unfinished. Her companion Dion Byngham was fortunately able to complete the book from her copious notes, during what he described as the first anguish of his loss.

Later, he wrote this Foreword.

Erma's intense inner life infuses this second volume of her autobiography, as it did all her thought and work: gardening, writing, and her embroidery and fabric pictures with their shimmering effects of colour and light. Her creativity led to the first volume of autobiography, *A Grain of Sand*, to a book on her herb garden, and to articles including one on how to "Make your own Theatre", which she actively demonstrated with her sumptuously-clad puppets and magically formed and coloured luminous Shadow Shows. She said that she aimed to see with an eye that missed nothing, and during the forty years we lived together I was sometimes almost overwhelmed by her sensitivity of vision, feeling and perception. That quality had been nourished and formed in Cornwall, and it is the development of her responsive spirit as she grew up in "Lyonesse" that is the subject of this book.

After Erma and I met, we spent the rest of the war at John Middleton Murry's community farm in Norfolk — about which she could have written another book.

The life at Lodge Farm, though tinged with the austerity of those times, had its compensations and pleasant moments, such as Harvest Suppers, for which Erma excelled herself by baking the most delicious vegetarian raised pie I've ever tasted. It had its grim moments too, as when, one Sunday morning, a drifting, abandoned, big bomber plane, clearing the thatched roof of Lodge Farm by merely a few feet, crashed in exploding flames, having narrowly missed obliterating us all.

Leaving Lodge Farm some while after the war's end was not without regrets. We then rented an attic from friends of mine near Rye. There, trying to resume embroidery work after the long interruption of the war was quite a problem for Erma; the shortage of materials reduced her to exploring the decorative possibilities of government-surplus sandbags and unravelled pan-scrapers, which, as she wrote in an article, "would unwind in shining threads to make hair and sun's rays and fiery nebulas". After a year in our attic we moved on to Dunshay in Dorset, at the invitation of Hilda and Mary Spencer Watson, the widow and daughter of George Spencer Watson, RA. They were good friends to us. Erma sometimes lent a hand in the mime shows Hilda performed in a barn theatre at the Manor. But her main focus was her embroidery and related art, which she varied by writing and gardening. There, too, we brought up our daughter Julia. It was a good life.

"A good life" . . . yes, though in those days we felt at times the sinister overshadowing of the recurrent Cold War climate, so that often we dreaded to see or hear the next news headlines. We could then only try to sustain each other by focusing on the remnants of saner normalities: the sweet spacial sanities of gentle fields and hills, wild flowers and trees were still around us and it was hard to believe they could ever be obliterated.

And meanwhile Erma continued her quiet, calming embroidery. Gradually, as resources improved, her work widened in style and scope and the sandbags and pan-scrapers could be replaced by velvets, silks and fine linens, and by real gold and silver threads. She became an active member of the Embroiderers' Guild, serving for a time on their Design Committee. In those years she had shows at Heals and Foyles Galleries and her work was sent on a round-the-regions tour by the Arts Council. So in her chosen field of fine-art embroidery she made her mark.

Erma did indeed have "magic in her eyes", implicit in the way she looked at and saw things. She had and was above all *a responsive spirit*, which found its focus in her creative love of beauty. That is what I was made most aware of during the many years we shared together. And one can discern it everywhere, growing and burgeoning in the pages of this book.

CHAPTER ONE

From Paradise to Coventry

Our moves from one part of Cornwall to another during the 1920s were invariably agitated and unexpected, and might more accurately have been described as flights; less like moves in the usual sense than hastily planned escapes from, or pursuits of, an invisible but dangerous enemy. But between the moves we settled and for a while, until a series of unfortunate incidents precipitated another sudden departure, we lived at Liskeard.

The house there had a garden and all the year round our doors and windows opened onto seasons whose changes were like changes of scene. Each in turn was a kind of gradual leave-taking, followed by arrival at a fresh destination, and I could never afterwards recall anything that happened during our stay in Liskeard without at the same time recalling the season. Even when events took place indoors and after dark, like a vast stage-set the season surrounded them. Blindfold, you could have told which season it was. For this you did not require sight; scent and sound were enough. Sounds from outside penetrated everywhere: the hum of

1

insects and bees in borage, rain whispering on leaves, and when the rain had stopped, the sound of water streaming down steep paths between raised beds. Then, in summer, there was the sound of church bells, as ringers from other parts of the country arrived by charabanc, headed for what was considered to be one of the finest peals in the Westcountry at the great church nearby. Always unexpected, the first sound would break across the sky like an annunciation and change the day to one of festival.

Originally a barn, the house had been used by the early followers of John Wesley as a preaching house. That had been in 1776 and only later had it been converted and built onto. One could never think of it as a house with a garden, but rather as a garden in which there happened to be a house. The garden came first. Even light had to pass through it before entering: an indirect side-light filtered through green leaves. It had been autumn when we came to live there, and that first year had been full of surprises, with glistening shoots shoving up from the muddy ground and green fuses flaring on branches above the sea of pink forget-me-nots, *Myosotis rosea,* which lay like a flood-tide around them. There were vines, and a fig tree whose moist green fruits tasted best when warmed through by the sun. The sheltered position, protected from every wind of heaven by high granite walls, was good for fruit-growing and induced an almost tropical growth. Masses of bindweed hung like aerial roots from half-strangled trees. Ramblers rambled up plum suckers and streamed down, still flowering, from the topmost branches, while unpruned shrub roses bore clusters which, far beyond reach, mouldered to scented dust upon the bough.

It had all defeated the previous owner, a bee-keeper who had struggled for some time to run it as a market-garden but, losing heart, had reluctantly sold it and shortly afterwards died. And it defied all my mother's attempts to eradicate the herby-scented blues and mauves, colours she disliked and which surged up everywhere. The garden appeared to be saturated by them: from the first blue of the periwinkles, planted as ground-cover, whose garlands festooned the paths all the year round, through drifts of lavender, borage and hyssop, to forgotten alkanet stretching up to the light through a tangle of dead brambles. The alkanet had forget-me-not-like flowers that did not fade or shed their petals but fell, still fresh, on the dead thorns surrounding them. There was an evergreen with pretty foliage all winter and in spring buds so dark that it was impossible to guess at their eventual colour, unless in fact they were to be black; it turned out to be a ceanothus. And in the greenhouse, *Didiscus*, the blue-lace flower: a bit of a rarity this — a blue variety of *umbelliferae*. In fact there were quite a number of out-of-the-ordinary little things. But a pile of old seed catalogues had been left behind in one of the cupboards and it was from their pages that the names and information concerning some of the plants were obtained. Long before the days of colour photography, they were lavishly illustrated with watercolour sketches of the flowers whose seeds were advertised. A combination of cornflowers and marigolds

3

appeared to be popular and figured more than once, carefully arranged in pottery vases.

Among some of the nicest things was a Spanish variety of love-in-the-mist which Harry Locke called "more love than mist" because of the large violet-blue flowers with red stamens; these later turned into spectacular seed-pods above feathery foliage that seemed scarcely strong enough to bear their weight. There was an ornamental corn whose swelling husks were visible through the papery leaves surrounding them, long before the coloured seeds and silks appeared. And purple clary, tall spikes of pale mauve flowers, each topped by a whorl of purple bracts through which, being borne so high, the light shone so that at times they looked like plants on which a flight of coloured insects had alighted with transparent wings.

At the lower end of the garden, damper than the rest, was a bed of my own favourites which the local people called Moses-in-the-bulrushes, or spiderwort; no less than four varieties, of white, purple, carmine and blue. From the catalogues one learned that they were "Osprey", "Purple Dome", "Rubra" and "Leonara", and that the real name was *Tradescantia virginia*, after John Tradescant, a naturalist to Charles I, who had brought it back with him from Virginia. In spring the first smoky sunset hues dyeing the green presaged the glory that was to come, and all summer long silky flowers stained picking fingers carmine and cobalt.

It was surprising how much always seemed to be going on through things simply seeding themselves, like the brilliant poppies — midsummer suns that rose blazing in unexpected places — and in what had been the vegetable garden, several rows of red orach, which the catalogues suggested could be equally well grown as an ornamental plant. When small they held raindrops in their coloured folds long after it had ceased to rain, but the grown plants were best viewed in the light of the setting sun which shone its level rays onto the tall seed-bearing spires and through the glistening leaves. It was then that the transparency so caught and held the eye. Of course the clary had it too, and the roses high up against the sky; but the orach most of all when at the sunset hour it towered like blazing glass. In an unformulated way one almost expected it to break, to shatter into a thousand pieces in a crash of jewels. Small wonder that I resented the thought of expulsion from this overgrown paradise.

Then there was the question of the school which I was now attending. As my mother's many prejudices included an objection to compulsory education I had never previously been sent to school nor, during an unusually isolated childhood, had I ever known the company of other children of my own age. So what I had come to think of as real life always seemed to be going on at a distance, within sight and sound but just out of reach, beyond the immediate area overshadowed by the figures of my mother and elder sister.

When, during our first year at Liskeard, the school attendance officer at last caught up with me I could scarcely believe my good luck and during the weeks of preparation that followed feared only that some disaster of unusual magnitude, some Act of God, would intervene to prevent my entering the mysterious and, to me, infinitely alluring portals of the School for Young Ladies in the centre of the town. Oddly enough this time coincided with the General Strike when a state of national emergency was declared, but the whole thing was over within a fortnight, after which everything went on as usual; and eventually the great day dawned.

They say that chaffinches reared in solitude have a very limited range of notes when they finally start to sing, and young monkeys deprived of the company of others of their own age show signs of confusion, throughout the whole of their lives. My range of communication was undoubtedly limited, and certainly no monkey could ever have been more confused than I was. But it was a bright confusion for life was at last coming within reach, along with the smell of ink and blotting paper and plimsolls. The sound of the school rising when the headmistress came in with the other teachers for Prayers, the opening and shutting of desks, the staccato note of a stick of chalk dotting Is and crossing Ts to me were like a symphony. What others took for granted were wonders to me on that first never-to-be-forgotten morning.

But this state of euphoria was to be brief, for within twenty-four hours a merchant seaman who had just returned to the town was found to be suffering from smallpox, and general panic ensued. At last the town-crier had something to cry about more serious than that the water-supply was to be cut off for a couple of hours. All the schools were closed; nurses and supplies of

6

vaccine were rushed from Plymouth; emergency innoculation centres set up; and all four local doctors, perspiring, and with rolled up shirt sleeves (the weather having become hot and sultry), worked all day and into the night. It was all so strangely similar to what I had dreaded, only much worse of course, for it had really happened. The older people could remember their parents talking about the dreaded cholera which had struck the town twice during the previous century. And of course something like that might happen again. If there was to be an outbreak of the disease, which everyone knew was possible, and many were to die, the school might never open again. But of course nothing like that occurred, though the poor seaman died. And within a short time the town was back to normal, what was ever afterwards known as the smallpox scare was over, and the school re-opened.

Started as a ladies' boarding school by a woman of refinement around the turn of the century, it had since changed hands and was now run by two Methodist ladies, Miss Pawley and Miss Merrick. It was officially known as Pencarrow House School for Young Ladies, though as often as not referred to locally as the Old Dame School. Situated near the Georgian Parade, its high slate-hung front faced two equally fine: that of the oldest house in Liskeard in which Charles I had spent seven nights after receiving the surrender of the Parliamentary troops further west, and the handsome Victorian façade of the Passmore Edwards Library.

The school buildings consisted of what had originally been two houses. The larger of the two contained the bedrooms and dormitories, kitchens, a mysterious region known as the servants' quarters, the dining-room and Miss Pawley's study, which opened off the gleaming hall. In the smaller were the Lower School and Infants' classrooms, the library and music room, and higher up, on the second floor, the Third Form room and two attics which were used as store rooms, one being entirely filled by the the boarders' trunks. A wooden annexe at the back of the bigger house, reached through a cloakroom on the first-floor landing, housed the Fourth and Fifth Forms. There was no Sixth Form.

The pupils were mainly the daughters of well-off farmers and tradesmen and most left at sixteen.

In a larger school I would have been lost, but life in my mother's house had been so restricted by rules and regulations, so full of pitfalls and taboos, so *fraught* that by contrast the life of this small school for girls seemed from the first to be very much simpler, and after a few preliminary difficulties I settled down fairly quickly. But for one incident, near the beginning.

I suffered from two slight disabilities. One of them was obvious, the other wasn't. I stammered, and also at times had difficulty in hearing what was said to me. It could scarcely have been called deafness, as I could hear the actual voices clearly enough, but sometimes the sound would become confused with a faint jangling in my own ears and I had to wait for this to pass. On the whole I had always managed to muddle along fairly well by watching people's lips and their eyes, which of course said so much more, though in rather a different way.

About a week after the school re-opened one of the boarders was found copying the solution to an algebra problem from another girl's homework and for this offence was to be sent to Coventry for a week; anyone failing to co-operate would herself be treated in the same way. Normally punishments for such things as inattention in class or constant carelessness in preparing work were meted out by the staff, but this case of so-called cheating was to be dealt with by the girl's classmates. Apparently this was a recent innovation introduced by Miss Pawley, who had come on the idea in a book by the Headmistress of Cheltenham Ladies College, and thinking that it would be nice to do things as they did them there (probably the sole point of similarity between the two establishments ever to exist), she had been pleasantly anticipating, if not actually hoping for, an early opportunity to try it out.

Of course I knew nothing of this arrangement, and when one of the Fifth Formers, putting her head round our classroom door, made the announcement concerning the unfortunate boarder, I only heard half of what she said — the first half — and not being familiar with the phrase she used, misunderstood it, though I thought it decidedly odd and rather drastic. Coventry seemed a very long way to have to go: one could only suppose that the girl's parents lived there. Or perhaps she had said Coverack, which of course was a good deal nearer. Seeing the girl at Prayers next morning I assumed that the trip had been abandoned, but she certainly looked very miserable and her friends appeared to be ignoring her. I felt sorry for her, and later in the day, colliding with her in the cloakroom doorway as I was leaving to go home and subsequently grovelling on the floor to help her pick up the books which I had caused her to scatter, I gabbled some sort of nervous apology while at the same time nodding and smiling with what I considered appropriate cheerfulness. After which I hastily sidled out, feeling extremely foolish because everyone within earshot had stopped talking and turned to look at me.

The sequel was immediate and inevitable, although at first I thought that I must be imagining it. No one appeared either to see or hear me and it seemed as though I had ceased to exist. It was first noticeable at Prayers the following morning. For though there was a shortage of hymn books no one offered to share with me until told to do so by a mistress, who noticed that I had none. Even then, the volume was held at an angle just beyond my reach and range of vision, and the owner did not appear to see me. Throughout the rest of that day none of the girls looked at or spoke to me, and lessons were almost a relief, for the teachers behaved as usual. At least, to them I seemed plainly visible. The curious thing was that no one appeared in the least vexed or angry with me. It would have been almost better if they had. No one had turned nasty; they had simply turned away. It was like being under some sort of a curse, and it was infinitely worse than being alone to be thus in company and yet unmarked, unrecognised.

During the morning break on the second day, seeing me standing alone, the mistress in charge asked me why I was not with the others, and my reply, "Because they can't see me", must have sounded almost imbecile.

Her own reply was cut short by a passing senior, who said something to her apparently in explanation, for after looking at me in some surprise the mistress turned away. Something really had gone wrong, something worse than anything I could have imagined and which I was quite unable to face. There was only one thing to do: get myself expelled as soon as possible. And for this no breaking of rules, no act of daring would be necessary, for at that moment the bell rang and as the others crowded towards the classrooms I made for the arched gateway in the high wall and was outside in an instant. No one had seen me go.

It was still two hours until lunch time and I did not want to go straight home, for when my absence was noticed it would be assumed that I had gone there and someone might be sent after me. So I made instead for the open country beyond the town through which a semi-circular detour would eventually bring me out near Castle Street where we lived. It was a strange walk, through lanes spangled with summer flowers and up a steep overshadowed track said to have been part of the old Roman way into the mining country. And in a strange way, almost pleasant, for the few people I met on the way spoke kindly to me, which proved that the pitiless spell or curse was powerless beyond the school gates. And I wished that I could go on walking for ever, or at least for a very long time. For while I walked I was immune, while I walked I was safe, while I walked I need not think of the future.

But inevitably it came to an end, and by the time I reached Castle Street I was rather alarmed at the thought of what I had done and unsure of how the news would be received at home. Dandelion seeds were blowing everywhere. Invisible because they were exactly the same colour as the pavements and road surface, only the pointed shadows showed, crossing and recrossing the ground before my feet as they turned and touched and turned again, now here, now gone. And there was something strange and uncertain about the sight of the shifting shadows, without at the same time the sight of what cast them.

My mother showed no signs of surprise on hearing my story, said absolutely nothing in the way of either sympathy or reproach, and scarcely appeared to be listening. But that evening she went to see Miss Pawley and some explanation and discussion must have taken place, for although the headmistress said that she found it very hard to believe that I could have reached the age of twelve without ever having heard the expression "to be sent to Coventry" and that my behaviour had been unprecedented she was, in the circumstances, prepared to have me back, adding that my shortcomings were by no means my fault but were due entirely to my *most extraordinary* upbringing: searing words for which my mother was never to forgive her.

I do not know quite what I expected to happen when I returned to school on the following Monday morning, for before the prospect my imagination had simply failed. Girls had to write a hundred lines for such minor offences as talking during class and so I would probably have to write at least a thousand for my unprecedented offence. And in addition to this, and very much worse, I anticipated the supreme disgrace of a public rebuke before the assembled school at Prayers. I had never witnessed this ordeal but had heard that no girl had ever survived it dry-eyed.

What actually occurred was so far outside the bounds of my fevered imagination that I thought at first I must be dreaming and would presently wake up to a harsh reality. For absolutely nothing happened. And although officially I was still in Coventry the situation was mitigated by friendly looks and smiles from my class-mates. I could scarcely believe it as the hours passed. Only towards the end of afternoon school Miss Pawley, passing close to where I sat, paused as though at an afterthought and spoke to me.

"Don't ever run away like that again," she said, "for if you were to we could never have you back". And no further reference was ever made to the episode.

It had been a painful five days, during which I had learned more about life than in the whole of the previous twelve years. One of the things was that sometimes in unexpected ways things that seemed to be going against me might in fact be working for me. For after this, really my third start (and, they say, third time lucky), my difficulties were noted, my seat in class changed from near the back to the front row to ensure that I heard what was going on and knew what was expected of me, and everyone went out of their way to help me.

Arriving as I had in the middle of a summer term, I had been temporarily placed in the Lower Fourth to see how I fitted in, which turned out to be rather unevenly. For while I got on fairly well with most subjects and very

13

much enjoyed English and Drawing, I was completely at sea with French and Maths. Ordinary arithmetic was bad enough, but geometry was worse, and algebra a nightmare. Now the end of term exams were approaching and I would have to take them, along with girls who had been doing these subjects for several years. Slowly, it was borne in on me that when the school restarted in September, I might very well find that I had been reduced to the Third Form, a prospect I did not relish; for not only would it be a decided come-down but the Third Form, at the end of a long corridor on the top floor of what was always called the Other House, was considerably less attractive than any of the other classrooms, displayed maps on the walls in place of pictures, overlooked an unbroken vista of rooftops and had, moreover, depressing associations connected with Friday afternoon detention.

Almost the sole form of correction meted out by the teachers was the imposition of lines, which consisted in having to write out such sentences as, "I must learn to keep my desk and locker tidy", fifty or a hundred times. It was possible to halve the time and effort involved in this task by fastening two pencils together, and this method had apparently worked very well until shortly after my arrival someone rashly attempted to use three, and was instantly detected. After that a new method was introduced which left no loophole for deception. Instead of the endless repetition of the same sentence, the requisite number of lines from Scott's *Marmion*, which we were studying in the English class, had to be written out, and in ink.

I can still clearly recall the look of the rather handsome book, and of the title-page:

MARMION
A Tale of Flodden Field

I thought it must refer to ground rendered sodden by flooding, a sort of bog in fact, and that it sounded very melancholy, as indeed were the opening lines of the introduction to the First Canto:

> November's sky is chill and drear
> November's leaf is red and sear.

Usually lines were done after school in one of the class-rooms in the Other House, which were empty and silent at that hour of the day, the day girls having all gone home and the boarders gone for their daily walk with one of the mistresses, or if it was in summer, to the tennis courts near the railway station half a mile away. Though it wasn't particularly pleasant, not the way in which I would have chosen to spend my time, it was not, on the other hand, all that bad either. And on the whole the new method was considerably less boring than the previous one, and at least helped to familiarise me with the poem.

But there was a further and more serious variation, the dreaded Order Mark with its accompanying detention. For some reason fifty lines, if incurred twice within one week, automatically carried with them an Order Mark and a further five hundred lines which, being so many, had partly to be done in school hours. The time chosen for this task was always a Friday afternoon, when the entire Upper School relaxed at a needlework class in the annexe, and the place, the Third Form room which was empty, the class having gone to join the sewing bee below. When more than one girl was involved they were forbidden to speak to each other during the time. And to be thus marooned, while the rest of the school embroidered and listened to a reading from *Lorna Doone*, the faint sound of which reached one's ears along with occasional laughter was hard indeed. I had experienced it once, during the first few weeks. But once was enough, and I never wanted to see the inside of the Third Form room again.

In the light of all this I anticipated the end of term exams with some concern. They started on a Monday and went on for the whole week. The English paper was to be the last, and one of the most important, as English was a compulsory subject for the Junior Cambridge Examination. Unfortunately, so were French and Maths in which I knew I had done very badly. My only hope as the week passed was that I might do passably well with the English essay, to which we were to devote the first two hours on the Friday.

There was an unusual solemnity and silence about that morning and the sight of desks with freshly filled ink wells and sheets of foolscap, as yet fair and unsullied, on which something might, just *might*, be written which would ensure my safe return to the Lower Fourth.

No exam papers were given out on this occasion and the two subjects, either one of which we might choose, were simply announced. They were "The Summer Holidays" and "Islands". I was bitterly disappointed. Of summer holidays I knew nothing; the words merely conjured up the sight of sandcastles and a few children in rompers on Hayle beach when I myself was a small child. And I had never seen an island, except for St Michael's Mount in the west, which was scarcely a proper island, being accessible along the sea-causeway from Marazion at low tide. And then I suddenly remembered that it had in fact been called an island, the Isle of Ictis or Mictis, by early writers who had also referred to the Casseritides, the Tin Islands, which were very probably the Scilly Islands, though others thought that the Scillies might equally well have been the original Avalon. Of course Ictis and the Casseritides alone wouldn't get one very far but, always an avid reader of legends and fairy tales, I could recall quite a number of islands half-real, half-legendary, like the Irish Hy Brazil which, though clearly visible, vanished when approached. There was one off the coast of Cornwall where women had worshipped the jealously guarded image of a Phoenician god, and I had sometimes heard my mother speak of the island of magicians, Eynhallow off the mainland in the Orkneys, where the Peerie Folk pastured their cattle in summer and about which there was a rhyme the children used to sing. And then there were the purely mythic, like the mysterious, turning island to which one of the early Grail Kings was transported, and those in *The Voyage of Maelduin*, one with a fiery wall around it and in the wall a door, through which the voyagers could see the beautifully-dressed inhabit-

17

ants drinking from golden vessels, and one whose walls yielded milk on ordinary days of the year and on feast days wine. Strangest of all was the Silver Meshed Isle, a four-sided column rising straight out of the ocean, with a silver net over the summit and a voice from the summit loud and clear: "but they knew not its strange tongue". Then there were those which men had invented . . . Treasure Island, Coral Island, Peter Pan's and Prospero's, with descriptions so detailed that I knew the terrain like the back of my hand. The encircling coral reef rising from rainbow waters, Cape of the Woods, Haulbowline Head, Kidd's Creek, the Valley of the Wreck; I knew them all. And though I felt pretty certain that none of this would go down very well with my teachers, least of all the bit about the maenadic Cornishwomen on what sounded very like Looe Island, and there was nothing to be gained by it, there was on the other hand nothing to lose either, for as far as I was concerned all was already lost. And once started, I managed to write pretty steadily, if in a sort of desperation, till the bell went just as I wound up with the rhyme

> Eynhallow fair, Eynhallow free,
> Eynhallow stands in the middle of the sea.
> With a roaring roost on either side
> Eynhallow stands in the middle of the tide.

The exam results were to be announced during the following week. Not all at once, but several each day, and more or less in the order in which they had been taken, so that the English results were to be the last, on the morning of the day before we broke up for the summer holidays. I had expected to come out rather low down in the class but as the marks were read out, starting as always with the lowest, I began to think that things were even worse than I had anticipated, as I did not appear to have been placed at all. In the end, I ceased to listen, as my ears had suddenly gone funny. And so I scarcely heard what was being said to me or understood why everyone, Miss Pawley included, was smiling at me or that in fact I was top, with ninety marks out of a hundred.

Though this was more than I had ever hoped for, I realised that it still might not be sufficient to counteract my poor results in French and Maths, and I spent the holidays in a state of considerable apprehension; needlessly so, as it turned out. For when the school re-assembled in September I found that, far beyond my expectations, I had been placed in the Upper Fourth. The windows of this classroom overlooked a part of the original garden that had been concreted over to form a playground (and around which a number of flowering shrubs had been left), and the sunken garden of the Other House with its palms and yucca and wide stone steps leading down to French windows. As it was the largest of the classrooms it was also used for the weekly needlework class as well as for the assembled school Prayers every morning, and for this reason contained an harmonium as well as a piano. There were splendid separate desks, too. In the Lower Fourth, we had had long ones designed to seat six girls, with only a narrow shelf beneath fixed tops on which to keep one's books, papers, pencil box, paint box and geometry-set. A variety of things were for ever overflowing and getting mixed up with those of one's neighbours on either side. The Upper Fourth had the added attraction of a flight of stairs which rose from ground level directly into the centre, and this meant that those seated in that area might suddenly find a head and shoulders slowly emerging through the floor between their desks, to be followed by an entire figure; usually a delivery man unfamiliar with the lay-out. This did not happen very often, but there was always the off-chance that it might.

Although recognised by the Board of Education, according to the prospectus, I never remember a Board Inspector visiting the school during the time I was there, and the standard could not have been considered very high. There was a resident music teacher, though, and piano lessons, which began each day immediately after Prayers, continued uninterrupted until four o'clock in the afternoon. Save for about half a dozen, including myself, all the pupils took music as a matter of course, so that anyone was liable to be called out of class for a lesson or to practise at any time during school hours. There was a constant to-ing and fro-ing between the classrooms and the music room in the Other House and usually one girl, if not two, were missing from the class, as piano duets were popular features of the school concerts. Satchels had to be left in the cloakroom but music cases were kept at the ready, within easy reach beside their owners' desks. There were no less than five pianos on the premises: the place rang with them. And though this was pleasant it was scarcely conducive to concentration.

Looking back on it now, I wonder that we learned even as much as we did from these ladies, who obviously regarded us as children from the first day we entered the school right up to the day we left at sixteen or seventeen. This tendency to look on us almost as infants showed in a number of ways. One was in the daily reading at Prayers, which, after all, was for the entire school, but which was not as might have been expected from the Bible itself, but from the pages of Arthur Mee's *Children's Bible*. Above the fireplace in the Upper Fourth hung a large colour reproduction of *Jesus Blessing Little Children* by Margaret Tarrant, and immediately opposite *All Things Bright and Beautiful* by the same artist, either of which would have been more suited to the walls of a nursery or kindergarten.

On our side, there was an unquestioning acceptance of authority. Treated as children, we were like children eager to please, and in return were easily satisfied. A look of approval was a wonderful thing, let alone a word of praise. Especially from Miss Pawley herself, a majestic figure who moved with a rich rustle, and whose elaborately dressed hair resembled a massive silver coronet. In fact, all the teachers were liked. Once, when a music mistress was leaving to take up an appointment in the north of England, a slowly moving queue of weeping girls filed through the music room to say farewell; in at the corridor entrance and out through the French windows into the sunken garden. I scarcely knew her myself, never of course having been taught by her;

but always anxious to join in anything that was going on, I wept with those that wept and added my tribute of roses and spiderwort to the already wilting mass of garlands heaped on, and beginning to slide from, the top of the piano. And, unnerved by this funereal scene of apparently uncontrollable grief, the poor woman herself began to cry.

But for my own part, it was not so much the teachers as my companions with whom I was most anxious to stand well, helpful and kind as they had been to me ever since the Coventry episode which, so traumatic at the time, seemed in the long run to have turned out to my advantage. There was a general feeling of friendliness among the pupils, and every new girl during her first term was allocated someone in her own form; "to help her settle down" I think was the phrase. I had originally been in the temporary care of a nice girl in the Lower Fourth who had helped me in a variety of ways and who, incidentally, could have instantly solved the sending to Coventry mystery had I only thought to ask her. Now, in the Upper Fourth I found that I myself had been chosen to assist a new girl who would be coming every day by train from St Germans where her father was village constable. We were to remain good friends for the whole of the time I was at the school, though the roles of helper and helped were very soon to be reversed. For Joyce did all things well, was that rare phenomenon, a good listener, and in addition was always ready to help with French homework or algebra or teach one to play "Für Elise". I remember her now with perfect clarity, while memories of some of the others are blurred and fragmentary, maybe partly because she seemed even at the age of thirteen curiously complete, in comparison to whom the rest of us had a long way to go and quite a lot to learn. Tall and thin, her short dark hair fitting her head like a sculpted cap, her gaze was unusually keen for a girl of her age, appearing at times almost to pierce whatever it was towards which she was directing her thoughtful regard. One could imagine her at every stage of her life and know that just as now she was good in class, she would later be a good wife, a good mother and even, hardest of all, a good mother-in-law.

Naturally she was a great favourite with the teachers, as was another member of the Upper Fourth, Veronica the star pupil. Star, because not only was she usually top of the class, played the piano well, was amiable and very pretty (contriving to wear even the school uniform with an air of distinction), but in addition she belonged to a well-known county family from whose seventeenth-century manor house she cycled the three miles to school every day. Miss Pawley obviously considered that her presence cast a desirable lustre over the whole establishment, and once in an English class when we came to the words, "The stately homes of England, How beautiful they stand", bowed towards her with the remark, "And yours is one of them". Occasionally Veronica appeared in the town on a Saturday morning booted and spurred, along with a handsome elder sister, both of them splendidly mounted. And sometimes she invited two friends to tea on a Sunday afternoon. Always two because of the long walk home later.

I can still see it now through the hazy autumn sunshine — the parkland and terrace and beautiful little clock-tower, and in the foreground Veronica, her pretty hair unplaited and floating around her shoulders, crossing the sward towards us. And later the family portraits and a Priest's Hole under the stone flags in the kitchen, and a languid mother who, vaguely sighting two unfamiliar figures in school blazers, asked, "Which is Hermia?" *Hermia!* I had never liked the name Erma but thought Hermia sounded quite enchanting and decided I would adopt it immediately. I also felt rather flattered that it was, by implication, this Hermia of whom this elegant woman had evidently heard and whom she now wished to identify, and not the other character, whose name was Dorothea. I went on to speculate that she might have been invited only because she knew the way, which I did not, and which was sweet and wandery but uncertain, through deep lanes by an old mineral railway track.

The two highlights of the autumn term were the annual Concert and Prize Giving which took place in October, and later the Christmas Bazaar organised by the school in aid of the British and Foreign Bible Society.

The day of the concert began with a brisk march in crocodile formation from Pencarrow House to the Town Hall at the other end of the Parade, and the exhilarating sight of the fine interior, enhanced by the heady herbal smell of the wax used to produce a floor-surface so glassy that one's first, though instantly checked, impulse was to slide. The morning was mainly taken up with a final music rehearsal. And as the function itself was billed to commence at three o'clock we had all to be in our places in the front rows by half-past two — a sea of blue above which our carefully tied hair-ribbons must have looked somewhat like a flight of agitated butterflies as heads were turned and necks craned in attempts to see where friends and relations were seated.

Chairs had been placed for the staff on the platform, which was decorated with palms, and a central high-backed chair with arms, more like a throne, stood immediately behind the table on which the prizes and certificates lay. The piano was opened and the music stands arranged for the singers. As the hands of the clock approached three silence fell. People stopped talking, the green baize doors leading onto the main staircase were softly closed and the seniors who had been ushering the audience to its seats took their places in the front row. There was no sound but the rather nervous footsteps of two late-comers; a knotted blind-cord, stirred by the draught caused by the sudden opening and swinging-to of the doors, tapped on a window glass. There was a feeling of almost aching expectancy, a tension like that of tuned strings.

Finally Miss Pawley, crowned with silver and robed in black, emerged with the other mistresses from an ante-room at the back of the stage and the proceedings began. These involved the presentation of the Junior Cambridge Examination and music certificates, school prizes for top place in class, and also a rather unpredictable Improvement Prize which always attracted a lot of interest, because it was for all-round improvement during the previous year and so, theoretically at least, open to anyone. In fact, it was not so much a case of finally being good enough, but rather of being bad enough to begin with, so that any last minute improvement would be sufficiently obvious to attract attention at the right moment. This year it had been awarded to a member of the Lower Fourth who, during the closing weeks of the summer term, with impeccable timing had suddenly ceased to blot her exercises or to incur fifty lines almost daily. She had also, overnight, learned to spell correctly and write with surprising legibility.

The distribution of prizes was interspersed with a variety of musical items — piano duets and songs, as well as recitations. The latter were very well received and had clearly been selected for the opportunity that they afforded for dramatic gesture, which was very much in vogue at that time. A niece of Miss Pawley's, a teacher of Elocution from Leicester, had recently visited the school and with head flung back and wildly flailing arms had pranced across our line of vision while declaiming extracts from *Christopher Robin*. Now, on this occasion, a third-former was twice recalled to the platform to acknowledge the applause occasioned by her spirited rendering of "Gillespie": "Riding at dawn, riding alone . . ."

The bazaar at the end of term was also held in the Town Hall and was officially opened by a local Methodist minister, acting in his role as secretary of the district branch of the British and Foreign Bible Society. As it was so near Christmas the hall was decorated, and this time a delicious smell of flowers and fruit assailed one on entering, and though the scent of the chrysanthemums predominated, that of the herby floor-wax ran like an undertone. Shopkeepers whose daughters were at the school gave lavishly to this event, as did the farming community, and there was a good variety of stalls for books, needlework, gifts, toys, groceries, farm produce, fruit and vegetables, and a cake stall with bread, splits, saffron loaf and pasties. As well as a flower stall, potted chrysanthemums were carefully arranged on display stands so carefully concealed that the effect was of solid banks of flowers. And immediately inside the green baize doors, against a backcloth of glistening flowers, the minister's wife presided over a stall selling shiny black bibles and literature relating to the overseas work of the Bible Society. Beneath the gallery, at the far end of the hall from the platform, three trestle tables covered with snowy white cloths were laid out with plates of buttered splits, saffron buns and slices of jam-sponge, while the tea itself came from three tea-urns worked by three Old Girls. Old Girls, as I came to realise later, were quite a feature of this occasion and were inevitably of great interest: figures originally so familiar to us, seen daily at close quarters and now belonging to another world, dressing so differently from what we remembered, talking so differently, distancing themselves from us with such (overheard) remarks as "the little school, Miss Pawley, in fact the whole set-up were positively unique, my dear".

Being the first bazaar of the season, it usually did very well and was considered a decided cut above the church bazaar that followed it a week later and which lacked the musical interludes, not to mention the needlework and gift stalls which were casually lumped together and labelled Fancy Work. It had an added advantage, too, in that unlike the concert, during which one had to stay where one had been put and remain silent unless actually performing, one could slip up to the gallery with a companion and admire the splendid scene below: friends and relations circling around the brightly decorated stalls, and Miss Pawley, swathed in black ornamented with jet which, from that distance and seen from above, sent out little flashes of light, slowly revolving while focusing familiar and not so familiar faces through her lorgnette and graciously acknowledging those nearest to her. In the gallery we were above the lights of the hall, and the scene wonderfully reflected in the great shining floor gave me the same feeling I had experienced on the first day of school: that of the bright confusion of life streaming swiftly past, but not too swiftly and well within my grasp. But along with this there always came the fear of losing it. At such times I would smooth the folds of my school uniform, and close my fingers tightly on the badge or tie or braid girdle as though for reassurance.

During the Christmas holidays I was invited to a number of parties. My mother disliked festivities of any description and so, although as a child I had always been given presents at Christmas, there had been no attempts at celebration, no exchanging of seasonal greetings or cards on the day itself, which was ignored but for the strictly observed ritual of Christmas Dinner. For this there was always turkey followed by plum pudding and cream, and because I was never allowed to leave the table until I had finished what was on my plate, the meal tended to last rather a long time. As a small child I had invariably wept and been sick on these occasions. As I grew older, I was merely sick.

I had never been to a party before, but now I was allowed to accept invitations. I acquired a party dress with a long sash, and was never to forget the sight of rooms transformed with brightly coloured garlands, holly, balloons and Chinese lanterns, or the light spilling through open doors into the wintry darkness outside. Usually two rooms were used: one for games and the other, in which there was the tree, for tea. The tables were lavish, with green, red, lemon and orange jellies in glass dishes, junket sprinkled with grated nutmeg in china bowls, bread and butter, jam and clotted cream, gingerbread, shortbread, bowls of fruit, and of course The Cake itself, elaborately iced and decorated and not cut till last, so giving everyone time to admire it.

There were usually crackers at each place containing small trinkets and printed riddles and jokes. The paper hats came separately and were quite a feature, every guest being presented with one on arrival and obviously expected to wear it for at least part of the evening. Fashioned from coloured crêpe-paper trimmed with gold or silver galloon and strengthened with thin card, some of them were really quite elaborate — crowns, tricorns, mitre shapes, and even some tiered and vaguely papal in design. And being reasonably strong, when not in use they could be folded and put away for next year along with the Chinese lanterns. As far as games were concerned, Musical Chairs and Blind Man's Buff were regular stand-bys, Musical Chairs coming first, well before tea and presumably to get things going while some of the guests were still arriving. Later on there was Pass-the-Parcel, Hide and Seek, Postman's Knock and charades. The great moment was towards the end of tea when the candles were lit on the tree, whose brilliance was then reflected in mirrors, glasses, what was left of the jellies, and in eager faces. Our eyes, alight with wonder, must have shone like stars.

CHAPTER
TWO

Harry and
the Elder Tree

It was during the following spring that certain sad events took place, events which meant that by midsummer the house at Liskeard had been sold and we were in full flight.

The house and garden had at one time been part of a larger property and still included several of the original outbuildings; among them, a stable which had been let to a road-mender to house the pony and cart in which he drove out daily into the surrounding countryside. In return for this facility the road-mender, Harry Locke, paid us a shilling a week, in addition to which he did odd jobs about the place, mainly outdoor jobs like clearing the overgrown paths, cutting back bushes and briars, and scything the long grass in the orchard.

Harry Locke had pale blue eyes and a gentle courtesy towards his fellow men. He lived, along with his large family, in a cottage opposite the church gate. Though he could neither read nor write, he expressed himself with a mild felicity, at times in a curious kind of rhythmical prose, and in an earlier age he would probably have become a balladist or rhymester, entertaining his fellows with his own verse and songs. For he had a fine voice and constantly sang as he went about his work. Staunch Methodist that he was, it was always hymns that he sang, making them sound less like hymns than his own spontaneous utterance; and both he and all his family were members of the chapel choir. Even my mother, not the most tolerant of women, could at first find no fault with him, apart from what she called his blasphemous superstitions, which included a belief in the Little People as the spirits of those who had died insane and not being bad enough for hell, having committed no crime, were on the other hand not good enough for heaven.

Born over sixty years earlier in a remote village on Bodmin Moor, he could recall the days of ill-wishing and overlooking, when every village had its wise woman whose spells counteracted such things, and the country people flocked to charmers for cures for warts and the wildfire (erysipelas), and consulted pellars if they suspected that they themselves had been begrudged or were victims of the evil eye. Pellars (or conjurors) were often the seventh sons of seventh sons; and on the whole they made the best charmers and were always to be found at fairgrounds and markets. As a boy he had seen them at Matty's Fair, the big fair held at Liskeard every October. And once he had seen a pellar's magic ring with its mysterious blue adder-stone formed by snakes hissing on hazel twigs. He had seen wonders, he had seen "the blood turned". And all these far-off things he "minded", so he said, as clearly as though they had only happened yesterday.

Early in the spring of the year my mother asked him to cut down an elder tree which she said was overshadowing the kitchen window and was suffocating us all. Obviously shocked, almost alarmed, by this suggestion, but reluctant to refuse flatly, he brought out all sorts of arguments against it. It was very bad, he said, to cut down an elder tree growing so close to, and obviously protecting, the house, especially after the sap was up: such action could only lead to trouble and to "the power against 'ee, not fur 'ee". No country person would do such a thing, knowing as he did the properties of a tree whose leaves, flowers, fruits, bark and even roots contained sovereign remedies against such a variety of ills, even against sadness itself, the twigs sometimes being used to transfer warts or a sorrow. Every countryman knew this. John Wesley had known it, and had prescribed elder tea for fever, coughs, toothache, palsy and a host of other ailments so numerous that in some parts of Cornwall people called it "the tea tree".

At most, he said, he would cut it back a bit. And all might have been well had he confined himself to a description of its medicinal qualities and its unsuitability as kindling; the Devil himself having been known to rise from the flames, it was never included by hedgers making faggots for burning. But unfortunately at this point, no doubt hoping to give weight to his argument, he spoke of those chopping an elder having seen blood stream from the tree instead of sap, being the wood from which Christ's cross was made. This of course constituted "blasphemy", a word which my mother applied to any theological statement with which she did not agree. And now, touched off on this almost fanatical religious point, she drove a hard bargain. Really, she said, lowering her voice, which during the argument had been peremptorily raised, it was all quite simple and she would not ask him again but leave it to him to decide. Either he could cut down the tree or he could look for stabling elsewhere.

This discussion, which took place on a Friday, left him little alternative and as no one worked on a Sunday, which was devoted entirely to chapel going, he said he would do it on the Saturday afternoon. He did not even stop to go home to dinner that day but ate the pasty and drank the sugary tea which his grandchildren brought him, sitting on the mounting block by the stable door. Once having made up his mind, however reluctantly, to fell the tree he set about it with his customary cheerfulness, every now and again breaking into the verse of a hymn as he chopped and stacked the blocks, as he called them. During the afternoon various members of his family looked in to see how he was getting on, though none of them offered to help, confining themselves to watching as though at the performance of some perilous task to which he alone was committed. It was obvious that they disapproved of the undertaking, and in spite of Harry's cheerfulness there was an unmistakable atmosphere as onlookers, talking in low tones, occasionally glanced towards the house.

My mother, who since getting her own way appeared to have lost interest in the whole affair, had remained indoors all day. But at about eight o'clock, as if for the first time becoming aware of the activity going on outside, she went into the garden to tell Harry to damp-down the bonfire he had made, at the same time calling out to my sister Mabel and me to close the windows before the place was "completely smoked out". Having closed a window, I stopped to look out at the scene in the garden where almost the entire Locke family were now assembled round a large bonfire. Harry had been building the bonfire for some weeks, waiting for it to be dry enough to light, and to it he had now added the sappy elder branches which crackled and hissed in the heat. Even Mrs Locke was there, tall and silent, watching with folded arms and wearing the spotless white apron without which she was never seen except in chapel on Sunday.

As I stood looking out, two things happened at once. My mother appeared round the corner of the house and at the same moment Harry, who was on the far side of the bonfire and had been feeding it, having just thrown on the last of the elder wood, stood back and with the rake with which he had been working still in his hand, held out both arms towards his family, his children and grandchildren on the other side of the flames, as though he would have embraced them. And then, raising his arms above his head, he broke into the opening bars of one of Charles Wesley's best-known hymns, at which his family joined him in harmony. The scene was so pretty in the twilight, with the bright faces around the fire, the wood smoke not rising but drifting away among the trees close to the ground, and the words of the hymn so sweet: "Let me to thy bosom fly", almost like a love-song, as the good old man conducted his beloved choir, that it seemed for a moment that something wonderful might happen, something mild and miraculous, some half-way meeting or act of courtesy. It even occurred to me that when she reached them my mother herself might join in too, and the strange day end happily after all. Instead, one by one, they turned and saw her and the singing died raggedly away as suddenly as it had begun. Within a few minutes the fire was dead, and the crowd around it gone.

Liskeard was always busy on Saturday nights, when people from the surrounding villages came in to do their weekly shopping on crowded and, in one case, horse-drawn buses, and the shops stayed open until nine o'clock. In the late evening the streets often became rough, with fighting breaking out among the men, many of whom by that hour were very drunk. Harry "belonged to" have a drink in the town on a Saturday evening. He usually went early and on the way home always looked in to see to the pony and pay the weekly rent. This evening he started out much later than usual. I was in bed by ten o'clock but I couldn't sleep and lay awake listening for his return. For when he came there might well be some reconciliation, some easing of the tension which had lasted all day. Of course the ripe moment had been by the bonfire earlier in the evening, but there was still another chance.

I do not know how long I lay awake, but I remember being very thirsty and getting up and going into the kitchen for a drink of water. As I was returning through the passage I heard the gate open and saw, across the window above the front door, a flash of light from the lantern which Harry always carried after dark, and thought that as always, he would go to the stable before coming to the house. But almost immediately there was the sound of running footsteps followed by a thunderous knocking on the door. And then it was flung open from outside and I saw Harry's eldest son leaning against the doorpost panting like a long-distance runner; a runner with a message, which he half-shouted, half-cried aloud. By then my mother had come out and I thought that it must be the flickering lantern light which at that moment made their faces so strange and terrible.

As he was coming home, Harry had been set-on by two men who in the darkness had mistaken him for their principal antagonist in a street fight which had taken place earlier. Later, at the Bodmin County Assizes, where they were sentenced to three years' imprisonment for Assault and Battery, their sole defence was to be mistaken identity. At first Harry was not expected to live, but he did recover, though he was never able to work again, and sat daily in his cottage doorway, one hand holding his pipe, the other restlessly wandering across the quilt over his knees, endlessly tracing and re-tracing the outline of the patchwork design he could no longer see. And when at last he was able to walk again he liked his grandchildren to lead him down to a certain spot in the town below, where, on the steps of the Old Market House, he could stand in the sun near the town clock, hearing the chiming and striking of the hours, and calling out to passers-by, turning in the direction of approaching footsteps the gentle, now sightless eyes which still remained the colour of summer skies.

It was very shortly after this that things began to happen at the house. Just "things", at first so vague and unrelated that we sometimes thought we must be imagining them. The groundfloor bedroom which my sister and I shared was at the back of the house and opened directly out of the sitting-room, where my mother slept on a type of couch that could be converted into a bed at night. One night I woke to hear what sounded like something being dragged across the bedroom floor, but as there seemed to be nothing there and the sound ceased almost immediately I soon went back to sleep again. I did not even think of mentioning it in the morning, but a few nights later the same thing happened again. A rustling sound, accompanied this time by distinct rapping, began under the dressing-table and then, crossing the linoleum, passed through the wall into the sitting-room, where it stopped by the window; this time Mabel heard it too and lit a candle. There was nothing to be seen, nothing to account for the sound which was totally unlike the noise made by rats or mice, the most disquieting thing being the way in which, without a pause, it appeared to pass through the dividing wall into the room beyond.

My mother, when told of the episode the following morning, dismissed it as a flight of nervous imagination, and to prove her point sat up for several nights in succession in order to listen. Nothing happened; and I at least was just beginning to feel that perhaps we had imagined it all, when one night about a week later we were all three wakened by a loud knocking on the sitting-room floor. After that Mabel and I were almost afraid to go to bed, but my mother insisted on treating it as something for which there must be a rational explanation, though even she was for the time unable to think of one. The sounds could easily have been thought to come from the large cellar underneath the house (which would have accounted for their apparently passing through the bedroom wall), but for the fact that the cellar door was always kept locked and the small window, which overlooked the back garden of a cottage into which the Lockes' eldest son had recently moved with his wife and children, was barred and did not open. Coal, drums of paraffin and gardening tools were kept in the cellar, together with an assortment of crates and seed-boxes; there was also an old tin trunk full of the usual "might come in useful" paraphernalia: sacking, pieces of old rope, bags full of rusty nails. And in the corner opposite the door the blocks of elder wood had been stacked.

After the night of the alarming knocking the sounds completely ceased for a time, but within a few days something else happened. The bodies of little birds began to appear among the blackened remains of the bonfire that Harry had made on that fatal evening. Of course one often came on a dead bird which a cat had killed and only partly eaten; but the birds among the ashes had not been mauled and appeared to have had their necks wrung (the local method of disposing of a bird caught in a strawberry net). Finally, one morning there was the remains of a dog, which must have been dead for some time as it was already in an advanced state of putrefaction. Unpleasant as all this was, it was not exactly mysterious, for these pathetic little corpses could have been left by anyone after dark, and there was really nothing at all to connect them with the nocturnal disturbances.

And then quite suddenly we all knew that something really was happening, something very strange indeed going on. For in the cellar, slowly but steadily, the pile of elder wood was diminishing, and this although it was not being used by us, and no one but ourselves ever went there. Quite suddenly it seemed as though the place was being invaded. Someone or some thing had access to it. And I remembered Harry's words when he was asked to saw the logs: "Bring in the elder, bring in the Devil!"

The cellar door opened outwards, and it was Mabel who thought of fixing fine strands of cotton from one doorpost to the other, high up where they would break when the door was opened, and of sprinkling flour on the rocky threshold, immediately inside where the footsteps of anyone entering would show. About a week passed, during which none of us went to the cellar, and as no more dead creatures were found in the garden and the night noises ceased and the threads across the doorway remained untouched, it really seemed as though the cause of these things had been settled, and that perhaps we could begin to forget about recent events and get back to normal.

The big Cornish coal range (the slab) was never lit in hot weather and during the summer months all our cooking was done on oil stoves. One morning before breakfast my mother, noticing that the glass reservoir of the double-burner cooking stove was low, went to the cellar for paraffin. And for some reason, perhaps because we had not been down there for a week or so, Mabel and I went too. I can see it all now: the strand of cotton wet with dew, sagging and faintly quivering in the morning air but still intact across the massive door. Even the padlock and the heavy chain twisted through the staples looked quite untouched. They had been spun around with a large spider web, and gossamers and lock and chain and staples were all wet with dew.

The first thing I noticed as the door opened was the smell of paraffin, but after that, almost at once, I noticed two other things. First, that the flour on the floor immediately inside was untouched and looked as fresh as when it had first been sprinkled; and second, that the corner where the wood had been stacked was empty. The logs were now piled alongside the paraffin drums. It was obvious that they had been saturated with paraffin, which in places had formed pools on the rocky floor. The beams of the ceiling also supported the ground-floor of the house above, and one match would have been sufficient to set the whole building alight. The place was a powder magazine.

On seeing all this Mabel burst into noisy tears; my mother, aghast, was for once speechless; and it was odd that it was I, never for a moment having doubted a supernatural cause for these events, who accidentally stumbled on a rational and very simple explanation. When younger, I had often played in the cellar and had always very much enjoyed the view of the neighbour's back garden, usually full of children, as seen from the little window. I had rarely looked at it since that time, but went over to it now. It was about eighteen inches square and constructed partly of glass, partly of the kind of perforated zinc which formed the sides of the large wooden food safes which were possessed by every cottage in those days. Deep-set in the two-foot-thick wall, sloping inwards at the top, at an angle like a standing photograph frame, shrouded in dusty cobwebs and barred on the outside, it looked very much as it had always done, save for the fact that the cobwebs now almost completely obliterated the view. I put out my hand to clear some of them away from the glass, and in so doing, I found that glass, zinc, bars and frame were leaning against the framework of cement which surrounded them on the inside. The putty on the outside had crumbled away and I could see that the entire window, complete with iron bars, had been fixed to the frame, not bedded into the granite walls on either side as might have been expected, and the whole thing could be easily lifted out, and as easily replaced, by any one standing in Harry Locke's son's garden.

I could never remember a time when my mother had not suffered from some form of persecution complex, constantly fancying herself (or at times all three of us) menaced, threatened, or beset. And this time perhaps she had some justification, though it is unlikely the Lockes ever intended actually setting fire to the house; more probably, distressed and enraged by the sight of their father's helplessness (both he and Mrs Locke now lived on the parish, which in those days was considered a disgrace for anyone under the age of seventy), they simply wanted to frighten the person whom they considered to be responsible for the tragedy. And if these happenings could be attributed to the supernatural nature of the elder tree, then so much the better.

Starting out for school later than morning, I found I could not get through the high double gates which led from our court into the street. Climbing on the wall in order to look over and find out what was preventing them from opening, I saw that the entrance had been wired up, and a notice bearing the words THESE ANIMALS ARE DANGEROUS, inscribed in large letters, had been fixed to one of the gateposts. Beneath these four words, like an afterthought, several others had been added, but these I did not understand, never having seen or heard of them before though I naturally assumed them to be of a disconcerting nature.

The episode caused considerable embarrassment, for my mother was forced to attract the attention of neighbours to whom she had not spoken for some time by knocking on one of their back windows, which overlooked our court, and asking for help. The husband having by that hour of the morning gone to work, and wire-cutters not being things normally left lying around the house like scissors, his wife had to go out in search of someone who might possibly possess a pair. By the time she returned with a man from a nearby furniture store a small crowd of interested spectators had assembled on the pavement by the gates. After that, things happened pretty quickly. By evening the property was in the hands of a local house agent, and a FOR SALE notice was on display outside, in place of the more sensational one removed during the morning.

For my own part, I did not at all relish the prospect of moving from Liskeard, where I had assumed we would be staying for some time, especially as I was now enjoying school there. I had always liked the place, built on rocky hills at the head of a valley laced with streams, and the ground which had been worked for metals by Carthaginians, Greeks and Romans as well as by the Phoenicians. Even its name intrigued: *Lys Ceruyt*, Court of Caradoc, as well as the names of some of the places surrounding it: Herodsfoot, Rilla Mill, Moorswater, Minions, Menheniot, St Cleer; names redolent of the Age of the Saints, of chantries, and ancient kings and springs and holy wells. To me it was simply a place where things could happen, and on the whole pleasant things; the sad episode of the elder tree had been an exception. It was always a place of possibility and promise, which perhaps no two people would ever see alike. Even when far from it in later years, though I knew that it really was a town in South-East Cornwall, on the junction of the A38 with the A39 as all the guide books said, it was also always a town in my mind, of my own imagining, a place where the outer world had at times accorded perfectly with my thoughts, and of course might do so again.

But at the last moment, and it really was the very last, for everything relating to the move was sudden and unexpected, it was decided that after all I would not leave Pencarrow House, but for the time being at least would travel to Liskeard every day by train.

I knew that the reason for this decision was not due to any unusual thoughtfulness on my mother's part, but solely to the fact that she did not want the bother of looking around for a new school, being, so she said, completely exhausted by her recent experiences with a series of unscrupulous house-agents. But whatever the reason, I was glad of it, for it was what I had hoped for but had hardly dared to expect.

CHAPTER
THREE

Saltash and
Angela Brazil

The new house was certainly very different from our two previous homes in the country — the cottage at Hayle and the converted barn at Liskeard — being one of a row of small red-brick Victorian villas on the hill below Saltash railway station. It was approached along a cinder-path running between the two roads which, parallel to one another, led down to the river and to the area of the town close to the shore that was known as Waterside.

The houses had been built during the 1850s, facing inwards to the steeply sloping hillside, with a complete disregard of the advantages the site afforded and at such an angle that, although the sun rose at one end of the terrace and set at the other, bathing the pathway and grassy bank in light, nowhere could its rays penetrate the shadowy interiors. And while in each house the view from the small back bedroom took in to the east the sweep of the river and the hills on the Devon side spanned by Brunel's great bridge, and to the west the vast expanse of the shining Hamoaze, the two front bedrooms and the sitting room merely looked onto the grassy bank rising precipitously from the cinder-path.

It was rather like living on the side of a railway cutting, an impression strengthened by the clouds of steam that hung continuously above our roof tops, not to mention the sounds that began early each morning and went on all day until late at night. Doors slammed, signals rattled, bells rang, and as part of our terrace lay directly under the end of the Royal Albert Bridge, the whole place shook whenever a long distance train passed through. These did not stop at the station, but slowed down on the bridge while crossing the river, then gathered speed as they approached the town. By far the most noticeable was the Cornish Riviera Express. Every morning it left Paddington, every afternoon, heralded by a shrill whistle from the Devon side, followed by a dull roar in the chimney, it set cups and saucers, doors and windows rattling. And then, looking up from the pathway, one could clearly read the legend — PADDINGTON-EXETER-PLYMOUTH-PENZANCE — as the great train thundered westward.

It all seemed a long way from the flowering wilderness and the birdsong and the pealing of sweet-toned bells. But at least it was easy to get away from, and I enjoyed my daily train journey to school. Several of the other pupils came from places along the line (including of course Joyce), and it was arranged that we would all travel together, which was much nicer than being on my own, and it was altogether finer to arrive and depart in this way and in company.

The walk to the station from Pencarrow House was especially pleasant on late autumn or winter afternoons. At that time of day things changed colour; shadows cast by the fading light, which would normally have been grey, when lit by the street lamps turned to pink or mauve or blue or a mixture of all three, the colours merging and the outlines wavering where the source of light itself was so variable. They speak of darkness falling but here, in the tender twilight, darkness rose as though it flowed from the Holy Well in the rocky hollow below, or from the cellars and underground tunnels with which the rock was known to be honeycombed.

From my point of view things were really turning out quite well. To be in a form with girls older than myself was of course a challenge and though each week I usually managed to come about third in the class, it required a pretty sustained effort on my part to stay there. Since beginning school I had started to keep a diary or, as I preferred to think of it, a Journal that I hoped one day would prove the basis for a book about Pencarrow House, something of a cross between a feminine equivalent of *Tom Brown's Schooldays* and *The New Girl at St Chad's* by Angela Brazil. During the summer holidays this ambition was considerably fired by a meeting with Miss Brazil herself.

Long before I went to school I had come on her works in the local library and been immensely intrigued by them. Although she wrote of characters whose home addresses included manors, granges, halls, abbeys, and even castles, the corridors of which were hung with faded tapestries and the rusting armour of crusader ancestors; characters who, away from school, inhabited drawing-rooms and "rose parlours" along with brothers home for the hols. from Harrow or Rugby, she was not unusual either in this or in her references to the "working classes", whose ranks included "devoted servants" and occasionally, as though by accident, "one of nature's gentlewomen". In all this she simply reflected many of the attitudes and prejudices of the day.

But she differed from other writers of school stories at the time in that the activities which she described, and even many of the adventures, were fundamentally simple, really a kind of making your own fun, and therefore available to anyone. Her characters wrote verses and stories, made music, produced entertainments, hunted for fossils, kept nature diaries, pressed flowers, drew and painted. Hair-raising adventures, hair's-breadth escapes, the finding of priceless treasure, all stand-bys with other writers for girls, were on the whole touched on but lightly, as were games, dormitory feasts and suspected hauntings. Nature formed an integral part of most of her stories, as Gillian Freeman was to note many years later in a fascinating study of her life and work, *The Schoolgirl Ethic*, when speaking of her passion for botany. One came on the little touches on every page, things like the difference between bugle and self-heal, and what is generally spoken of as winter heliotrope being given its Latin name *Petasites fragrans*, in every way more descriptive.

And then the sense of the spirit of place in her books set them apart. She described surroundings fully and lovingly, in sharp contrast to other writers in the same genre whose schools were mainly located in unidentifiable terrain anywhere in the country. I had been delighted by several of her Cornish settings, with Chagmouth, obviously Polperro, in *A Fortunate Term*, and Porthleven in *The Head Girl at the Gables*, and by the enchanting evocation of the north coast of Cornwall in *The School by the Sea* in which the school grounds, situated at the head of a two-mile-long promontory, contained a spring dedicated to a Celtic saint on whose Feast Day the youth of Pontperran, Porthmorvan and Perranwrack had been wont to try to learn their fortunes by divination until such times as the event had developed into such "a riotous and undesirable ceremony" that the public had been excluded. Here surely were echoes of the Padstow May Day hobby-horse revels?

This fascinating blending of fact with fiction greatly appealed to me, and I secretly cherished the hope that I might eventually become the author of similar works myself. By way of preparation for that distant day I had written several stories, but though each was neatly copied out and stitched into a brown paper cover when completed, it had never occurred to me to speak of, much less show, them to anyone. For the time at least I was content to work in the dark, and no doubt I would have remained so indefinitely, but for an incident which occurred a few days before I went back to school.

Although my mother rarely played the piano it was always kept at concert pitch and was tuned regularly every few months though never, as far as I can remember, to her satisfaction. Being as usual dissatisfied with the piano tuners who came from the music shop in

Plymouth, she had sent for one from Polperro, someone she had heard was also a teacher of music, and consequently better in every way, Gilbert Morris. A piano tuner who was also a piano teacher was unusual; one who had been not only a "child prodigy" but also a pupil of the famous Lazare Levy, head of the Paris Conservatoire, and was now himself while still young a composer and concert pianist of some renown, was quite remarkable. On his first visit to the house at Liskeard he happened to pass the open door of the room in which I was scribbling at the table and asked me what I was doing. Reading my opening paragraph, he said that a friend of his, Angela Brazil, wrote school stories, too. On hearing of my unbounded admiration for her works, he suggested that I might like to meet her. The sequel to this was an invitation from Miss Brazil for my mother, sister and me to have tea with her at Polperro. And this event, first postponed because of the smallpox scare and later for a variety of reasons, one of which was her return to the Midlands for the winter months, was at last, over a year later, to take place during the summer holidays.

I wished I could take a friend with me. Preferably Veronica, whose ancestral connections would undoubtedly appeal. Or Joyce, whose background would be equally interesting in another way. For in the stories fathers and uncles frequently figured off-stage as magistrates, and the author was obviously on the side of law-and-order. Ideally, we should appear in school uniform and carrying satchels, in which case our hostess could not fail to be struck by our resemblance to those figures depicted on the dust-jackets of her latest works,

51

now currently on show in all the book shops. In a way we were her creations, her word made flesh, as though her characters, like prototypes, had come first and we were but fashioned in their image. At heart we were all *The Girls of St Cyprians*, *The New Girl at St Chads*, *Monitress Merle*. But neither Joyce nor Veronica could come, and full uniform being worn only in term time, I had to be content to appear in my blazer over an ordinary dress.

It was quite a thing in itself to be going beyond Looe to Polperro, when Looe itself always seemed to mark the end of the journey. After circling a rocky amphitheatre in the hills that rather splendidly echoed and amplified the engine's whistle, the branch line from Liskeard to Looe turned down through a wooded valley of lead and silver mines, rushing streams, and lanes as deep as small ravines, to follow the course of the East Looe River as far as Looe. Here in the lower reaches its waters met those of the West Looe River, forming a vast lake at high tide twice a day. And it was not difficult to see how the town had got its name, *logh* or *loe* being the Cornish word for an inlet of water. Everywhere along the river Himalayan balsam grew in great profusion and to a height of six feet, the flowers that ranged through every shade from smoky pink to claret glistening on crimson stems. Perpetually rustling, with the sound of their ripe pods exploding to scatter the seed like spurts and bursts of shot, the great plants seemed alive and restless.

At Looe we caught the bus to Polperro. The cottage was reached by a steep path and a flight of stone steps leading up the almost perpendicular cliffside. Everything in the pretty room seemed to melt into and blend with everything else, including Angela Brazil, a nice-looking woman in mauve voile who, after an initial greeting, scarcely glanced in our direction, moved and spoke very slowly and gave the totally misleading impression of being rather vague; misleading, because as I realised later, she actually missed nothing. There were bowls full of pale pink and white roses everywhere, and round the walls a number of her own watercolours in narrow gilt frames, mostly landscapes done abroad in Switzerland or Italy. The overall effect was of taste and delicacy, and extremely harmonious. My mother and Mabel were seated near the tea-table but I was given a low, cushioned stool by the window. In this position I did not know quite what to do with, or where to put, my feet that seemed suddenly to have grown larger, but I did have an uninterrupted view over the town and harbour, which from that height made me feel slightly dizzy.

I had taken it for granted that the young composer, Gilbert Morris, would be there too, probably accompanied by his fiancée, a tall elegant girl whom he had brought to the house at Liskeard one day very shortly after his first visit; but they did not seem to be expected, and Miss Brazil presently spoke of him not so much as one would of a highly valued friend (which he undoubtedly was) but more as one might refer to a highly valued possession. At one time she had attempted to adopt him, an offer which he very understandably refused, having reached the years of discretion and having heard some of the conditions involved (which included adopting the name of Brazil). Maybe this detail

53

had escaped her notice or she simply chose to ignore it. Perhaps at heart she was rather cold and valued people less for themselves than for their gifts, in this case, the brilliance of one whom the gods had richly endowed. After his first London recital at the Grotian Hall the previous year she had made a scene when he had chosen to attend the small celebration arranged by his parents and some friends, in preference to accompanying home Dr Marie Stopes and herself.

In some ways it must have been a rather uneasy friendship but, like many such, also a fruitful one. He was a constant guest to whom she read long extracts from, and with whom she discussed, "work in progress" and much of her work was obviously derived from their relationship. She emphasised the single-minded dedication necessary to a musical career in almost every book, and in one was to deplore the case of a young composer who left every composition unfinished (although the ensuing fragments were obviously the work of a genius), and whose periods of wild ambition never lasted long enough to carry him through the whole of an opera.

Gilbert did have an unfinished opera based on the Arthurian legends on the go and this, given her love of Celtic mythology, must have been near to her heart. But here any hint of a resemblance ended; the character in the book, after marrying the daughter of a baronet who straightaway disowned her, fell under the influence of bad companions, lost all his teaching pupils and died broken hearted "in the prime of his youth, the success he had dreamed of still unwon". Gilbert on the other hand was to marry his lovely gentle girl and live to enjoy a long and interesting life. I myself saw him rarely, but I was to think of him ever after as someone who once did me the greatest kindness.

It was a very good tea, with an unusual variety of sweet biscuits circulated in a blue and white Wedgwood biscuit-barrel from which, when it was finally placed within my reach, I was told to help myself. The talk was of this and that. I remember something being said about our original arrival in the county ten years earlier after a seemingly endless journey from Liverpool, the dark city where, as my mother remarked, "even the flowers had soot on them". Gilbert had mentioned Angela's insistence on her name being pronounced Brazil (the first syllable as in Basil), the same as in Hy Brazil, the magic island off the coast of Ireland from which returning travellers were for ever after known as "Brazil" or "Blessed", and from which she liked to think her name was derived. And we were careful to observe this preference.

She put me very much at ease by looking not at, but past me; and she seemed interested in Pencarrow House, especially when she heard that some of the girls came from Looe and other stations on the line, along with brothers attending the Grammar School at Liskeard. She asked how many pupils the school took, and up to what age. On hearing that most left at sixteen and that in the case of girls wishing to stay on to take the Senior Cambridge Examination they no longer had to attend classes but worked alone in the library with a mistress, she thought it an excellent thing: "*most* interesting, more like studying with a private governess". The early teens were the best part of one's schooldays, she said — the magic years, a highwater mark before being beset with the necessity of passing exams. And it was incidentally this fourth-form age group of and for which she wrote.

I was immensely flattered by this interest and, writhing on my velvet stool as I turned alternately from the figures by the tea-table to look out through the window, below which the ground simply fell away, I began to feel rather light-headed. To everyone else in the room I knew it was not a very important event, a day like any other. It was a big event in my life. And by the time we rose to go I felt I had truly had my crowded hour. Or rather, one and a half hours; for having arrived at three o'clock we departed at half past four, one and a half hours being considered the correct duration for such a visit.

My mother and Mabel having gone out through the open door first, I was about to follow when Miss Brazil turned and for the first time looked at me. And then, her last words wonderfully ringing in my ears, I too was outside sliding down the slippery slope. We saw her again (almost an anticlimax), half an hour later when walking on the hill on the other side of the harbour. Now wearing a light summer coat and shady straw hat, she appeared to be vaguely drifting uphill. Catching sight of us, she raised both her hands, in one of which was a little bunch of pink and white roses, and pointing upwards she said something, which may very likely have been about the beauty of the day. But her words were completely drowned by the cries of the gulls which, swirling overhead, cast circling shadows on the ground around us and throught the clear waters of the harbour below.

The following summer *The Little Green School* was to appear and be described as the most Cornish of all her books. The first chapter contained the account of a family arriving at Restormel in Cornwall after a long journey from the commercial city of Winchpool in which "the very flowers in the park had soot on their leaves". Here they changed onto a branch line which followed the course of a river as far as the small seaside town of Port Erbyn. Later, settled on the off-shore Dinas Island where they were one day visited by a vaguely familiar figure in the shape of a brilliant young pianist who "played delightful music for a whole hour", they attended a small local School for Girls, the upper divisions of which were compared to "a collection of private pupils studying with a governess". There were references to brothers attending the Grammar School and to a Seminary for Young Ladies, both situated at Lestormel which, being on the main line and "a market town . . . served as an educational centre for a considerable area of smaller places". Liskeard, Looe and Looe Island were instantly recognisable.

At the end of the summer holidays I re-entered Pencarrow House, determined to become its chronicler, naturally inspired by the visit to Angela Brazil and by her parting words, almost those of one writer to another: "Good luck with the writing", which made me feel that a corner of her mantle had fallen on me. (Kind Gilbert Morris had evidently told her of my literary aspirations.)

What I had in mind was a history of Pencarrow House, bringing it up to the present day: fact generously laced with fiction. But this would obviously have to wait for some time. It occurred to me that meanwhile the time might be usefully spent on a shorter and less ambitious work, which could then be submitted to the editor of one of the weekly or monthly magazines for girls, who would inevitably reject it. One had to begin somewhere, and I knew that most authors at the start of their careers went through an initial stage during which their work was returned, and that rejection slips were part of a real writer's life, so much so that the thought of receiving them myself was positively exhilarating. Also, by adopting this method I could perhaps get the initial stage over and done with before, at some distant date and with reasonable hope, I started work on the Pencarrow House book.

With all this in mind I began at once on a story. But as there was always a lot of homework to be got through during term and it still required all my efforts to keep my place in class, it was not finished until the spring. By that time it was a good deal longer than originally intended, for in a way it was easier to write a long story than a short one. I liked to pause, not to run on too quickly, and if the scene was outdoors, to try to describe the light and where and how the shadows fell and what flowers grew by the way; maybe because I liked to read of such things, as in Angela Brazil's own books. On such points she never disappointed, never glossed over; but lingered on the pollen haze, the January hawkweed flowering bravely in sheltered places, the purple paradise of neglected lilac bushes, and the rockpool at the verge of the high tide when the water, catching the colour of the setting sun, turned to wine among the corallines and sea spleenwort.

Once I had finished, it was simply a matter of submitting my manuscript to an editor and awaiting its return, the length alone, over eight thousand words in longhand, almost certainly making it unacceptable.

Originally I had rather fancied the idea of sending it to the monthly for which Angela occasionally wrote, *The Girls' Own Paper*. This magazine was considered superior to its rival *Schoolgirl* and to the weekly *Schoolgirls' Own*, which was printed on pulp paper, in ink which smelt deliciously like freshly spread tar and came off on one's hands. Its range was rather wider than that of the other papers. The Archbishop of Canterbury had written an article for the first Christmas number, deploring sectarian rivalries, within the Christian community; and as well as stories there were always a number of features on subjects like the League of Health and Beauty, and the Margaret Morris Dance Movement. Camping, rambling, hiking, Youth Hostelling all seemed popular, and physical fitness a positive fetish with this magazine which, as late as 1937, was to publish an enthusiastic article in praise of the Hitler Youth Movement, describing the German Girls' League as "the greatest in the world". On the whole it was rather too arduous for my liking, with its emphasis on sport and the great outdoors, and it was devoid of any botanical interest; I do not remember any mention of plants or even of scenery, landscape being treated merely as a backcloth against which energetic figures rambled, leapt, marched, lit camp fires or pursued a ball.

The other possibility was *St Dorothy's Garden*, an attractive magazine for young people of both sexes, which we had originally come on in the SPCK department of a Plymouth bookshop. Published and edited by the Anglo-Catholic vicar of a church somewhere off Ludgate Hill, and the official organ of a society founded by this enterprising cleric and known as The Young Crusaders, it was extremely well produced. It had a cover design by F.I. Noble, well known as the illustrator of a series of books by the naturalist Marcus Woodward. The drawing depicted the saint in her garden, and the late summer flowers were instantly identifiable, as were the birds which came to her hand for food and the butterflies surrounding her halo. Despite an obviously religious bias (the stories usually concerned the life of one of the saints), it covered quite a wide range of subjects: gardening and nature notes and a regular feature on Arts and Crafts, which included embroidery, barbola and stencilling. A Christmas issue had published a one-act Nativity Play along with diagrams showing how to cut out the costumes, and an article on how to make a Christmas crib from coloured paper and cardboard. There was, too, a regular monthly alphabetical guide to architectural features and church furniture, including vestments, which had just reached M, with Monstrance, Morse and Maniple. Compiled by the editor, this was illustrated by F. I. Noble, as were the gardening and nature notes. Quite obviously my story did not fit into any of this, but one had to start somewhere and I finally got it off to the London vicarage, along with the stamped self-addressed envelope for its return which I felt pretty certain would not be very long in coming.

It was not returned. Instead Father Sankey wrote to say that he would be pleased to publish it as a serial in six monthly parts, and that although it would not be illustrated each instalment would have as a heading a tail-piece by Miss Noble, who would be getting in touch with me as I might have some suggestions to make regarding the designs. As it was unusual for a story of school life to be written while the author herself was still at school, and the readers would be interested in this, he himself would be writing a short introduction.

At Pencarrow House, where I had acquired some cachet from the visit to Polperro, my friends now seemed to be almost as surprised and pleased as myself, and the news soon spread through the school. I was anxious not to attract the attention of the staff to the affair, knowing quite well that they were unlikely to appreciate my vision of a school for girls situated in the middle of Bodmin Moor on the haunted site of a medieval monastery, even if the place should shelter treasure hastily concealed at the time of the Reformation. Nor would they relish the fact that this school was run by liberally minded women who not only tolerated midnight feasts but at times positively encouraged them, despite the fact that such events frequently followed moonlight excursions through the Arthurian territory around Dozmary Pool, from the waters of which the apparition of an arm brandishing Excalibur occasionally appeared.

But a farcical situation was soon to arise. A third-former whose father worked at the local *Cornish Times'* offices mentioned the story at home. A repon:er arrived at the school and the following week the paper carried an article headed "Cornwall's Young Authoress", which compared the event to Marjorie Bowen writing *The Viper of Milan*, a popular best-seller of the day, when she was only sixteen. It went on to say that the author of the now eagerly awaited *Treasure of Langorran* was even younger and that her future career in the literary world would be watched with the keenest interest. *The Western Morning News* copied the feature. And the *Cornish Guardian*, who sent a journalist from Bodmin, produced a considerably longer article; this, accompanied by a photograph and a number of inaccuracies — among them, a statement that the introduction was to be written by *Judge* Sankey — was to appear later. Unfortunately all this time no one had read the story or even part of it. And the first instalment was to quickly dispel any illusions as to its literary merit, although it looked very nice, with a beautifully-drawn garland by F.I. Noble of fern fronds bright-cut on a dark ground surrounding the title.

Even at the time I could not imagine how such an effusion had come to be accepted, unless it was because of something towards the end, when three fourth-formers exploring a series of worked-out slate caverns in search of the royal fern *Osmunda regalis* accidentally stumbled on the much-sought treasure: church plate; illuminated manuscripts (vellum not being perishable like paper); and, perfectly preserved under several layers of stone-dust, a priceless collection of richly embroidered vestments that only required a little light brushing-down in order to reveal the arms of an Earl of Cornwall in silver thread. Maybe Father Sankey considered that the recovery and consequent detailed inventory of such valuable ecclesiastical artifacts went rather well with his own monthly notes on church furniture (from which I had obtained the names of several of the rarer items that shone through the blue slate-dust at Langorran). But of course I never really knew, just as I never knew what my teachers thought of the work, though I sensed that at least one of them, Miss Merrick who taught English, considered the whole thing rather absurd. Of course she was right; but as she also considered much of *Jane Eyre*, from which she was reading to us on Friday afternoons, absurd, I had known that I was unlikely to escape her criticism. Having dismissed Mr Rochester as a fervid creation of almost pure fantasy, she also pronounced *Villette* "scarcely feasible" as an account of life in a girls' school. Miss Pawley had ordered copies of *St Dorothy's Garden* for the school library when she first heard of my story but after the first instalment came out did not refer to it again and, rather to my relief, it was never to appear on the shelves.

It was a nice library, with lots of poetry, and a discreet selection of Dickens, Scott, Mrs Gaskell, and Robert Louis Stevenson. There was no Angela Brazil, no L.M. Montgomery, nor Susan Coolidge's "Katy" books; and one felt that *Little Women* must have somehow slipped in by accident when no one was looking. As well as the usual children's classics there was Norden's *Topo-*

graphical and Historical Description of Cornwall, with fascinating little drawings and maps, and one of the few copies still in existence of the rare 1856 first edition of John Allen's *History of the Borough of Liskeard*.

I liked this book very much, for the life going on every day in the streets through which I passed seemed to meet and merge with the life described between the dark brown covers. And I dipped into it whenever possible. "Dipped" was the word, for the book was too precious to be lent out and so I could only see it during a morning break when it was too wet to go outside, and then only on request, as only fifth-formers were allowed a free run of the library. I liked to read of former happenings, as when the shock of an earthquake was felt in the town for three seconds on July 15th, 1757, and an observer saw "multitudes of blood-red rays converging from all parts of the heavens to one dark spot". And of the rider who came to the ruins of the castle where Richard, Earl of Cornwall, had sometimes lived, and afterwards wrote, "And moreover, in the front of the castle-wise moonstone gate or portal, I beheld his arms cut in stone . . . within a bordure bezantic, a lyon rampant, crowned".

The earliest authentic mention of the town concerned the freeing of a female slave around the year 1000, when priests from the Priory at Bodmin "came in procession to LYSCARRYUT bringing with them the sacred bell of St Petroc" for the ceremony before witnesses. I know I had come on this story somewhere before, for I well remember waking early on the morning of the first Good Friday after we came to Liskeard and hearing the sound of a bell followed by a cry. This was repeated at intervals, sounding at first far off and then more clearly, as though slowly approaching through what was already a brilliant morning. The sounds, sweet and rounded, might almost have been part of a Litany, an impression emphasised by their repetition and the ringing of the bell. And I thought, "It is all happening again . . . they are coming, the Holy Ones, bringing the bell of St Petroc, their long shadows trailing like robes behind them through a spangle of spring flowers . . . they are coming up the valley." Only when at last quite near did the words finally become audible and resolve themselves into "Hot cross buns! Hot cross buns! Four a penny! Hot cross buns!" It was the first time I had heard the cry, for in the west the bakers had always sold the buns straight from the shops on Maundy Thursday.

All travellers from the fourteenth century onwards mentioned the spring in the rocky hollow, the "ever flowing and health-bearing fountain of excellent water" around which, as around a core, the town had first grown. "The Well of Lyskerit" had never been known to run dry or even low, and the waters were said to possess healing virtues and a certain stone nearby "magic properties". It was commonly known as Pipe Well, probably because of the four piped outlets through which the water flowed into a granite trough. The sun never penetrated to the alleys and lanes around the well. A region of perpetual shadow, it was usually deserted and silent but for the purling water, and very cool even on the hottest day.

Little plants grew in the crannies of the walls, and in early summer alkanet flowered among the stones, dropping its bright blue flowers some of which, caught in cobwebs, shivered in the faint air current above the water. I liked the spot and had frequently taken a short cut through it on my way to school in the days when we lived in Castle Street. And often in after years, on hearing the easy, "Oh yes, but of course we know Liskeard; we always drive through it on our way to — we know it well," have wanted to say, "You have not seen the rocky hollow, and in the rock a well, and nearby the well a stone, and by the stone a flower called alkanet — evergreen alkanet, right at the centre of the turning world — the flower that does not fade. Unless you have seen these things how can you *know* Liskeard?"

CHAPTER
FOUR

London Visits and a Local Election

At the time I little guessed that it was to be my last year at Pencarrow House, and for this reason I was completely unprepared for what followed, though later I was often to think of the words of the song which we were then practising for the school concert:

> As torrents in summer suddenly rise
> Though the sky is still cloudless . . .

As far as I was concerned, the sky of that last summer was all but cloudless, for it was a meaningful time with, so it seemed, "everything going for me". I thought that I knew what Angela Brazil had meant when she spoke of "the magic years", and that it was rather like what Harry Locke implied when he said, "the power was fur 'ee and not against 'ee". As though borne along by a strong current, I was able to look a little way ahead and anticipate, if not invariably good things to come, at least interesting things. Everything mattered, and up to a point at least, almost anything was possible.

But it still took me all my time to keep up with the rest of the class in some subjects. Because of this I was always very anxious to avoid missing any time at school and would conceal any slight ailment such as toothache or a sore throat for as long as possible in order to attend. I was also unable to appreciate our annual visit to London, which always took place in the middle of the summer term, solely in order that we could take flowers to the Cenotaph. Apparently only red roses would do, and for this reason alone it was imperative that the visit should be arranged during the flowering season of what was always referred to as "the Scarlet Pillar", a red rambler, cuttings of which my mother had brought from the garden at Liskeard. She had planted them along the narrow verge of the cinder-path at the foot of the grassy bank and in this position the rose had flourished, its thorns leaving barbed tips in the bleeding flesh of those unwary passers-by who, pausing to admire, unsuspectingly touched it. Spreading almost menacingly in all directions, in places along the ground, and rambling up, over and through anything encountered on the way, including a neglected buddleia which it clothed in sinister splendour, its progress was more like that of a fiery dragon than a plant.

Naturally, these absences were not regarded favourably by Miss Pawley, to whom my mother wrote in her characteristically high-handed fashion that they were a necessary part of my education; a subject to which she had previously given singularly little thought. The excursions were a source of painful embarrassment to me, as it was I who had to lay the flowers at the foot of the monument. Seeing people bow towards it and men uncover their heads as they passed, I took it to be not a memorial but the tomb of a whole multitude of warriors, which, as a tomb, must extend downwards even farther than it rose, spreading like a vast catacomb beneath Whitehall.

It was usual for visitors to London, up from the country or from overseas, who had lost someone in what was always called the Great War, to leave flowers at the Cenotaph. My mother had lost no one, but as she always said that had she borne six sons she would have gladly sacrificed them all in the service of King and Country, the occasion was treated with the studied solemnity of an important public engagement and always took place on the morning following our arrival in town, immediately after viewing the Changing of the Guard at Buckingham Palace; by which time the blooms that had been cut early on the previous day had begun to wilt and shed their petals in small red flurries.

The first time had been just before I started school, when I had never seen traffic any heavier than that in Liskeard on a market-day, which, apart from a few small vans, was mainly horse-drawn. Approaching the great monument alone, my mother and Mabel having remained on the pavement looking on, I tightly clutched what I held with both hands. My instructions were that after depositing the flowers I must on no account turn my back to the memorial but must reverse down the shallow steps and then, still without turning, back across the road and onto the pavement, all this in the very teeth of the traffic. I can still remember the feeling of almost uncontrollable panic and how at that moment I hated the great city, the noise of the traffic, which had started off the jangling in my ears, the heat and the sight of the dying roses and the blood on my hands.

Of course it was never afterwards to be so bad. And although I never ceased to be embarrassed, I later came to accept it as an inescapable endurance test, to be got through quietly and with as little fuss as possible. Once it was over, I knew it could be safely forgotten about until next time. For from the very first it was obvious that this curiously isolated incident bore little relation to anything I was likely to encounter elsewhere, and none whatever to the number of wounded ex-service men whom one saw every day in the streets selling matches, playing mouth-organs, or sometimes in small groups singing to the accompaniment of a concertina or old violin, their ragged caps laid down for pennies in the gutter at their feet. My mother never gave them money, saying that once one started one would never know when to stop, there were so many of them; and so of course there were: everywhere in the streets and squares, outside the theatres and the entrances to the Underground stations, at the foot of the steps leading to galleries and museums.

They were different from those street musicians who, simply classed as beggars, sang hymns and popular songs of the day in the towns and villages of the west and who, though ragged and often lame, being weather-beaten from a more or less compulsory outdoor existence, looked somehow stronger and less vulnerable. The figures in khaki had medals but sometimes no hands or eyes; mostly they sang the kind of songs that everyone knows from childhood, the kind called Old Favourites, interspersed with war-time songs like "Keep the Home Fires Burning", "The Roses Round the Door", and "Goodbye Dolly Gray".

Every day, everywhere, from early morning until dark these songs were in the air all around, like the incidental music to some film of the streets. One was rarely without them for long, for no sooner had the sound of one singer or group faded into the distance than another began. The first time we went to London I thought this strange music beautiful but almost unbearably sad, and could not understand where these soldiers came from, for they were obviously not connected with those in Whitehall, who I knew had all died in the Great War, part of a victorious army, a kind of nobility. These sad men in the streets had apparently fought elsewhere, in other battles and another war which, I thought, they must have lost. But they seemed to be as much a part of the seething city as the traffic, the policemen on point-duty and the palace guards, and like them were evidently taken for granted.

My mother constantly complained of my lack of response and intelligent interest on these occasions, and with some justification, for from the moment we arrived at Paddington station I counted the days and finally the hours until our return. Unable to relate anything I saw to anything I knew, I was totally preoccupied with comparing things seen to things remembered, for instance setting the shine of the Crown Jewels against those to be won at the hoop-la kiosks at Matty's Fair. For as the best of jewels was their light, and that mostly came from reflection, the jewels in the Tower fell far short of the "fairings" at Liskeard, which at dusk reflected starlight and later, naphtha flares and all the blaze of the fairground. It was a sort of groping around for the reassurance of the familiar. My greatest source of comfort were the geological galleries at the Natural History Museum in South Kensington, where alongside glistening fragments from the lead and silver mines of Cornwall I could read the splendid names and know that the places actually existed, and that I had not imagined them, nor merely dreamed a dream of Herodsfoot and Silver Valley and Goonzion.

However, there were to be two unexpected highlights during these excursions. The first had occurred the previous summer, when we had gone to London immediately before moving to Saltash (to catch the roses at the peak of their flowering season before the cuttings were taken), and had visited Pollock's Toy Theatre Shop in Hoxton. From my point of view this was an outing with real meaning and purpose. In the school library, looking through a recent copy of *The Teachers' World*, I had come on an article describing what was known as the Juvenile Drama, as well as Robert Louis Stevenson's famous essay, *A Penny Plain and Twopence Coloured*, about the little paper theatres with printed sheets of scenery and characters based on successful London plays and Victorian and Regency pantomimes, each sheet costing "a penny plain and twopence coloured". I had been greatly taken with the description of the dim little shop "close below St Paul's . . . low in the roof and smelling strongly of glue and footlights" and with

Stevenson's words, "If you love art, folly, or the bright eyes of children, speed to Pollock's . . ." For this treasure house, this Aladdin's Cave, still existed at 73 Hoxton Street, N1.

"Close below St Paul's . . ." was scarcely an accurate description of the shop's whereabouts, and we had to take a bus to Shoreditch and then follow the conductor's instructions for reaching Hoxton Street, bearing left by the big church and then right. It was less like part of a London slum than a town in the country; not unlike some of the back streets in Hayle or Redruth. The horses and carts and big brewers' drays filling the roadway, the shouts of the drivers, and the women in coarse aprons in small groups calling out to one another, everyone knowing everyone else and nobody hurrying, may have had something to do with this impression. It seemed a hundred miles from London, and thinking of it even now it is as though I was remembering a street where, just out of sight beyond the houses, were fields.

The shop front of Benjamin Pollock's Theatrical Print Warehouse, next door to the Adam and Eve pub, was exactly like the Victorian print that had been reproduced in *The Teachers' World*, apart from the name, which at one time had been Redington (Benjamin Pollock having married a Miss Redington and taken over the business from his father-in-law), and the numbering, which had been 208 and was now 75. Inside, it was very much as Stevenson had described it; it still smelled of glue and of the colza oil which, used in tin containers with wicks, served as footlights. It also smelled of onions frying in the back room, through the doorway of which Miss

Louisa Pollock appeared, wearing a little blue velvet toque, with a brisk, businesslike "Yes?"

The shop's dimness was part of its attractiveness, for even on this bright summer morning it held a cave-like twilight through which the tinselled theatres shone like constellations and mock suns. They were everywhere, even hanging from the low ceiling, just as they had done when Stevenson bumped his head against one all those years ago; in fact anyone of above middle-height would have had to dodge in order to avoid them. There was a bewildering variety of plays and pantomimes with their accompanying books of words, as well as a selection of all-purpose drop-cloths and side-wings which could be used for any play, and spare sheets of Harlequinade and Pantomime figures. The sheets still only cost a penny for black-and-white and twopence for hand-coloured.

My mother made some remark about the number of interesting and appreciative visitors they must have had over the years, many of whom had gone away to write about the shop; not only Stevenson but Ellen Terry, Gordon Craig, Bernard Shaw, Chesterton, to which Miss Pollock indifferently replied, "Oh, we get all sorts," and then in the tones of one referring to the notably eccentric, added, "Mr Diaghilev and Mr Sitwell!" Throughout the conversation she kept disappearing into the back regions, probably to keep an eye on her cooking, as it was near lunch time.

I chose mainly penny plains, not only because money invested in this way went twice as far, but also because in the painted sheets crimson lake and Prussian blue predominated along with the green known as bice, and I wanted to choose my own colours, along with plenty of the gold paint sold in twopenny containers, and the gold and silver tinsel supplied for decorating the costumes.

Finally I came away triumphantly with a splendid Regency-type theatre proscenium, which only required mounting on cardboard to strengthen it; and to my mind, two of the most beautiful plays, *Timor the Tartar*, and *The Silver Palace*; and two pantomimes, *The Sleeping Beauty in the Wood*, for which there was a wide choice of scenery and a special drop-curtain showing Princess Beauty asleep in a scallop shell, and *Jack the Giant Killer*, based on the Cornish legend of the giant of St Michael's Mount. The opening scene showed the giant asleep on the rocks at the foot of the Mount with a church spire tucked under one arm. As well as Jack and Giant Blunderbore there was a fine array of colourful characters: Adelgitha, a Princess of Cornwall, Fairies Dazzelbright and Goldenglisten, Harvesters, Villagers, Jolly Tars, Goblins, and "Schoolgirls" in billowing gowns and quite startling *décolletage*. The production also included a special sheet of "tricks": a strip of "Harlequin's Pictures", to be drawn through the previously cut-out clouds above what was presumably Marazion beach, depicting the figures of Lord Nelson, Shakespeare, and less illustrious characters with names like Dandy Jem, Dusty Bob, Artful Dodge and Inch-of-Mischief.

Stevenson, too, had preferred to colour his own plays. Writing that with "crimson lake (hark to the sound of it — crimson lake — the horns of elf-land are not richer to the ear), with crimson lake and Prussian blue, a certain purple is to be compounded which for cloaks especially, Titian could not equal", but that "when all was painted . . . all was spoilt". For the purchase and the first half-hour at home was the summit, after which the interest declined, and he spoke of the tedium, the worry, and the long drawn-out disenchantment of an actual performance. I did not find this was so at all and managed to colour, mount, cut out, and muddle my way through a performance of *Jack the Giant Killer*, which, probably mainly due to its Cornish associations, went down very well with an indulgent audience of fellow fourth-formers.

I coloured and cut out most of the sheets, all but *The Silver Palace*, which to my mind was too fine to be treated casually, and if done at all would have to be done rather splendidly. I thought the scenery, Neptune's Crystal Palace, the figures of Tritons, Watersprites, Firedemons, and the principal characters Coral Crown, Quicksand, Ironspark, Volcano the King of Mount Etna, and the Blue Eyed Maiden, Lady Lumina, wonderfully beautiful. The colouring alone would have to be something very special. No bice green; but jade green and emerald along with turquoise blue, ochre and *coral* pink which was not difficult to mix, pearly white and a lavish use of gold and silver. If a Silver Palace couldn't have lots of silver, what could?

For a performance I would obviously have to have help with the voices, as some of the lines were truly rousing, like "Take thou these swords of magic power," and "Hark! The wild tide gushes, our task is o'er; Speed, brother speed, to the crystal palace shore." I got as far as colouring the first scene but left it uncut, though I occasionally took it out to look at and admire; and I very much liked to think of it, to recall it at odd moments while waiting for an algebra class to begin or for the morning train, an encrusted image like a little icon around which I could think and plan. About some things one could afford to be patient, and this was one of them. Sometime, someday, somewhere there would be a glittering performance; meanwhile there was no hurry: it could all wait.

The Hoxton episode had an unexpected sequel a year later, when on the visit to London during a June heat-wave our inevitably rather feverish cultural activities included a visit to the Diaghilev Ballet. It was a Wednesday matinee and all I could think of was that back at Pencarrow House Miss Merrick would be taking the Upper Fourth for botany, one of my favourite subjects, and that I was missing it. In addition I had a special reason for wanting to be there, as on the morning of our departure I had noticed near the railway line, just beyond the end of the station platform at Saltash, a mass of what from the appearance of the little forked manikin-type flowers I took to be the man orchid. This of course constituted quite a find, and I was naturally eager to impart this interesting information. In fact the plant was twayblade, but I did not discover this until later.

The atmosphere in the crowded theatre was stifling, and the names of Ballanchine, Lifar, and the Maryinsky ballerinas Trefilova and Spessivtseva meant nothing to me.

The third and last ballet after the second interval was

The Triumph of Neptune. Lost in thoughts of the man orchid and the fame my discovery would bring to the school, (the Natural History Museum would undoubtedly require photographs of the plants and an account of the discovery), I had not read the programme I had been given to study and so did not know that the *décor* for this English folklore ballet, a theme originally suggested to Diaghilev by Sacheverell Sitwell, was "based on the popular cut-out lithographs for Pollock's toy theatres". But the curtain rose and I was never to forget my first sight of the opening scene from *The Silver Palace*, resplendent in more or less my own colours — emerald, jade, turquoise, ochre and coral, all flourished with silver, and far surpassing my imaginings. The ballet itself was lovely, rather like a pantomime only without the silly jokes and songs and funny men dressed up as women and red-nosed clowns who fall off the stage into the big drum in the orchestra pit. There was a beautiful Harlequin like a spinning top, with wonderful *twisting* leaps at the start of his dance. And my enthusiasm for the production, coming as it did after the usual torpor, went some way towards mollifying my mother, for the time at least.

After we got back to Cornwall there were still about six weeks of the summer term left, for which I was glad. There was a general election that year, and it was a lively time. I do not know what elections were like in other parts of the county but at Liskeard, for weeks beforehand, there was a feeling of mounting excitement, culminating in an almost carnival atmosphere during election week and on The Day itself, when the results for the South-East Cornwall (Bodmin) Division were announced and the successful candidate proclaimed to the awaiting crowds from the balcony of Webb's Hotel on the Parade. Feeling ran especially high this year for although the town itself was a Liberal stronghold the Tories had won the seat at the last election. In any case, it was always a pretty straight fight between the Liberal and the Tory; the Labour candidate scarcely counted and always lost his deposit. Only some of the unemployed men wore a red ribbon, and I never remember seeing any red window decorations.

The Liberal candidate was the famous Isaac Foot, a Plymouth solicitor and a man of great humanity and learning, whose book collection of over 70,000 volumes was considered to be the largest private library in Britain. He had been Member for the Bodmin Division in the early twenties but had lost his seat in 1924, and was now standing again. Known as Our Isaac, or even Sir Isaac by many who considered that he deserved the title, he was immensely popular in the district, and well known. At one time he had lived at St Cleer, a village on the edge of Bodmin Moor, whence he had daily walked the three miles to Liskeard station, declaiming poetry as he went. He always liked to read aloud when walking and said that he had come to measure distances by reading.

He was uncompromising on the questions of Free Trade and Teetotalism, which latter policy lost him a good many votes, the brewers feeling that carried to its logical conclusion, it might very well lead to the closing

79

down of the pubs. A Methodist local preacher, his Liberalism was closely linked to his religion; was in fact synonymous with it. Mrs Foot was said to have regretted that none of their sons, although successful in other fields, (Lord Caradon, Baron Foot, Michael and Sir Dingle), had been good enough to become a Methodist minister. She was referring not to moral goodness, but to the fact that their preaching might not have been considered good enough for a profession which had always regarded eloquence as the first essential. Isaac himself emerged well on both counts, a truly good man and also an orator whose preaching was such that at the close of a sermon congregations felt like rising to applaud. Many church people, including Sir Arthur Quiller-Couch, went to chapel especially to hear him; an otherwise unheard of procedure in the days when there was a very definite division between "Church and Chapel."

During the week before to the election the local tradesmen and shopkeepers finally relinquished any attempt at neutrality, their shop fronts lavishly decorated with blue and yellow bunting and windows displaying large VOTE FOR FOOT posters amidst a flowering of silky blue rosettes with gold centres.

Their public meetings were conducted with the same enthusiasm, and the streets rang with their campaigning songs.

> If you want to find Our Isaac
> We know where to look
> We know where to look,

Right at the top of the Poll
You'll find him,
Right at the top of the Poll.

And the rousing

I'm going to vote, vote,
Vote for Isaac Foot.
He's going to win,
He's going to win.
You can hear the people roar
That we'm going to put him in.

The other parties must have had their songs too, though I never actually heard any of them. There was a good deal of verbal abuse on both sides. Party colours were torn down and there were scuffles in the streets, the Tories enjoying the dubious advantage of feeling free to get drunk on these occasions, if a little extra courage was required, although when sober they usually confined their activities to spitting at or in the faces of their opponents, including those of the Foot family themselves. Their Association headquarters, a tall, narrow house in the centre of the town, was unmistakable even in what one might have called peace time, someone having had the bright idea of painting it in the Party colours. The front door was black and yellow and the black-framed windows curtained in yellow.

A brisk social life centred around these eye-catching premises, where a large room on the first floor was used for whist drives, socials and, more recently, concerts.

This was mainly due to the enterprise of the Party agent for the area: Prater, a large, perspiring, backslapping *It's all go* character in his fifties, who usually appeared in tweeds and "loud" waistcoats (sometimes black and yellow), and was generally known as "a very good fellow". He was unmarried and lived in a small villa on the outskirts of the town with his mother, to whom he was devoted and whom he invariably described as "my Ma". Everyone, irrespective of their political outlook, liked "my Ma", a tiny, friendly, good-humoured lady who was always very carefully dressed and who made her own hats: little crochet toques and "tammys" decorated with flowers or pompons or sparkling hatpins. How deep her political commitment went no one knew, but she was obviously happy to go along with anything which involved "Sonny", as she called him, of whom she was obviously immensely proud.

The Association's social activities were mainly organised by a small Entertainments' Committee, consisting of half a dozen ladies said to be devoted not so much to the Conservative cause as to Prater himself. This seemed to be especially so in the case of the indefatigable secretary, Miss Moyle, a stout lady in her late forties, with carefully permed grey hair and slightly protruding eyes. She was a close friend of Mrs Prater's, with whom she often went on shopping expeditions to Plymouth on Saturdays, partly in order to help the old lady, who as well as being rather deaf was extremely absent-minded and left to herself would as likely as not have boarded the wrong train on the way home and found herself "up Tavistock" instead of at Liskeard.

The concerts were an innovation, originally thought up by Prater, and were very popular. A music teacher — a widow — and her eighteen-year-old daughter had recently come to live in the town and had joined the Association; spoken of as "gentlefolk who had come down in the world", they were considered great assets. The daughter had a good voice and both she and her mother could be relied on to help arrange and to perform at any musical function. I can't remember their name but the daughter was always known as "Cherry Ripe", owing to her spirited rendering of the song, a stand-by encore for all occasions, and to her wearing cherry-red, a shade which suited her. I never spoke to her but had sometimes seen her at a little distance through a shop window or in the street. She walked lightly with a springing step. In fact all her movements were light, swift and restless, as was her glance which passed from face to face, from this to that, without ever lingering. Very slender, almost sylph-like, she somehow appeared in perpetual motion. Even when waiting to cross the road or to be served in a shop, she would tap the ground with one foot, her heel partly withdrawn from the shoe or, humming to herself, lightly drum on the counter with her finger-tips.

During this particular campaign the Association was to suffer considerable embarrassment, caused by a scandal which was of no less public interest (possibly more) for being a mystery. Initially at least, no one appeared to know what had actually happened, beyond the fact that it had taken place "on the actual premises", great efforts having been made to conceal the nature of the offence from the opposition, who might very naturally have been expected to make capital out of it. They were in fact already circulating stories that suggested a large consumption of drink on the premises at all hours, verging on conditions of "riotous assembly", though it is doubtful that even the fiercest of them really believed this, as the Association was conducted along extremely law-abiding lines, mainly by respectable middle-aged ladies, and the premises were locked up by nine o'clock every night. Only the caretaker, Prater and the secretary had keys, which included master-keys to the storerooms and lavatories as well as all the offices. I myself did not know what really happened until many years later, when I was told the story.

Miss Moyle, who had been working late at the office as she often did, had heard strange noises coming from the Ladies' lavatory on the ground floor. Thinking that someone had been taken ill and receiving no reply to her concerned calls, she used her master-key to open the door, whereupon she was confronted by Prater and "Cherry Ripe", both in a state of *déshabille*.

Afterwards she said that she had no alternative but to act as she did, and promptly, "in the interests of all decent women and the good name of the Conservative Party". Of course, from one point of view both good name and interests might have best been served by the silence for which Prater was said to have implored her, but she obviously felt otherwise, and having made up her mind, in her usual businesslike fashion, she lost no time. An emergency meeting was called the following day, the divisional headquarters contacted and a deputy agent appointed. Prater immediately disappeared from public life, and both he and his mother very shortly afterwards from the town. Some attempt having been made to conceal the true state of affairs from Mrs Prater, the old lady's bewilderment was extreme. Sonny had told her only that he was to be posted elsewhere, and with supreme irony it was Miss Moyle to whom she finally applied for a fuller explanation of recent events. She had made the secretary a little good-bye present in the shape of a crochet raffia hat, similar to one of her own which Miss Moyle had often admired in the past, and she took it to the office herself.

The election results were announced on the day after the voting, and coming out of school that afternoon several of us went along with the crowd, which was sweeping past Pencarrow House on its way to the Parade. The Liberals had won by a large majority, and in a way it was felt to be as much a Methodist victory as a political one. Some people openly wept for joy, and when someone started to sing a hymn known to be a great favourite of Isaac's,

> O Beulah Land, Sweet Beulah Land,
> As on thy highest mount I stand . . .

Those around took it up, the mild breeze bringing the sounds close to one's ear and then carrying them away to where they were drowned by the cheering. He came out on the balcony of the hotel then, brushing the coloured streamers from his light grey suit, tall and very distinguished looking, and at that moment pleased as he waved to the people below and stood waiting to speak. It was a pleasant scene in the summer sunshine, the fine buildings and multi-coloured crowd very much like an Impressionist painting in milky colours to which whorls and ribands and a scattering of bright dots had been finally added in blues and gold.

The town remained restless after the election was over, and probably as a result of it, not for any political reason but because with the relaxing of many habitual restraints during the previous weeks it had been unusually lively. Now people still continued to sing in the streets (although no longer the campaigning songs), and to laugh and shout to, or at, one another. This was most noticeable among the out-of-work men and boys who normally stood silently at the street corners but who were now heard to murmur, laugh, whistle and call out after passers-by.

One young unemployed man who seemed especially affected by this mild form of midsummer madness was a character known as "Pincher" Quick who had a deaf-and-dumb wife, seven children and an emaciated whippet; the dog was devoted to him and followed him every-where, more like the shadow cast by a wavering light than a real animal. While it was well known that Pincher ill-treated his wife and children, it was equally well known that he would have shared his last crust of bread with the dog, and was in fact kind to animals in general. Humming away in what sounded like a strange language, he would kneel down by any stray dog or cat he encountered, after which the animal would fawn on him and try to follow him. A story went round that by means of this curious, almost hypnotic humming he had cleared a farmer's barn of the rats with which it was infested, all other methods having failed.

Normally Pincher eked out his fifteen shillings a week dole money by doing a bit of gardening (he was good at this, being said to have green fingers, though totally unreliable as to working hours and given to digging by moonlight), and by gathering wood and selling it in bundles as kindling. Small, dark and thickset, with bloodshot eyes in a face suffused with red, as if from over-exposure to some fierce source of heat, he was never to be seen at street corners watching the world go by with the other out-of-work men, but only when hurtling around the town, always wearing plimsolls and closely followed by his dog, their progress swift, silent and to all appearances, purposeful.

I encountered him once while we were still living in Castle Street, when having taken a short cut past the Pipe Well on my way home from school, I had stopped to pick some of the blue flowers. As usual the spot was deserted, and I was just thinking how silent it was but for the little song of the waters, although in the centre of the town, when I was startled to hear the words, "What you got there 'en, you?" spoken quite close to my ear, and turning, saw Pincher on the step above me. Although he had come so silently, he was panting as though from running, which seemed very strange and alarmed me even more than his hideous grin.

"It's alkanet, isn't it?" I said, feeling foolish and frightened; and dodging round him, I made for the lane leading up to the street above.

"Oh 'ark the 'erald angels sing; couldn't say I'm sure!" he called out after me, took a few stumbling steps in my direction and then stopped.

After that, on my way home, I was careful to keep to the streets where there were plenty of other people around. I had rarely seen him since, and then only in the distance. But now, unexpectedly, Pincher was suddenly very much in evidence again: his attention focused, for no obvious reason, upon Pencarrow House itself.

Although the front overlooked the wide thoroughfare leading onto the Parade, the school entrance, which was also the tradesman's entrance, was several hundred yards away in another street. It was approached along a rather dark covered passageway that ran between the buildings on either side and led into a small "court", in one wall of which was the school gateway. This court was actually the backyard of a cottage belonging to an old lady whose husband had recently died, and whom Pincher had undertaken to supply with firewood. This showed a nice helpful spirit on his part, or would have done had not so much of the wood been green: not gathered but torn and split from the tree, and still leafy. And some of it was elder, which as a countryman he must have known was practically useless for burning, although he persisted in scattering the sappy branches around the yard in considerable quantities.

His deliveries were carefully timed to coincide with that hour in the late afternoon when the day girls were leaving and the school gate, which was normally closed, stood open, affording anyone standing at the old lady's cottage door an uninterrupted view of the school premises and a close look at everyone coming through. His lively interest appeared to cover all age-groups, starting with the Infants which included boys up to the age of eight, little groups of whom he would hustle together and march briskly along the passage and across the road outside: a wholly unnecessary procedure as there was scarcely any traffic passing at that time of day.

This had been going on for some time when Pincher changed his tactics. On the far side of the street from the passageway and almost directly opposite to it was a gap between the houses where a track led to the cattle-ground, deserted save on market days. Pincher now took to haunting this area, where it was possible to linger indefinitely, keeping an eye on the school passage opposite without attracting the attention which such behaviour would have done in the street. On the emergence of any girls he would hastily cross over, fall into step beside them and scurry along, at the same time attempting to engage them in some sort of conversation. He waylaid Joyce and myself several times in this way, and remembering the blue flowers from the previous confrontation with me by the well, offered to show us where more of the same plants grew in great profusion along with many other interesting varieties. This unsuspected garden of delights apparently lay just beyond the cattle-ground at the head of a narrow gully; into this gully the surrounding waste land drained, rendering it inaccessible save by a devious way known to himself alone. As the entrance was hard to find, being almost completely smothered by thorny roses and lovelies-bleeding, it would be necessary for him to come to show us the way.

On several occasions when he had obviously been drinking, his account became even stranger. For unbeknown to all but himself, he said, it was the garden of the "small people", the *muryans*, those who had died mad and so, not good enough for heaven nor bad enough for hell, surged everywhere among the thorny roses, hoping for a chance to be reborn into the world of humans. Almost invisible, as small as the ants among whom they lived, they could fasten and feast on human flesh wherever a thorn had pierced it and drawn blood, secretly thriving to finally emerge and be mistaken for ordinary children. And as such they lived, though for ever muryans at heart, seeing and hearing more than ordinary children do; seeing into the future, knowing the thoughts of animals and insects, hearing the grass grow.

Looking back on it in later years, I often wondered that we were not more frightened by him than we were. But, his startling imagery wholly lost on us, we found his attentions more disconcerting than alarming, and simply hoped that one day they would cease as suddenly as they had started, preferably before the autumn term began, as we would not relish the thought of his company on the way to the station, or tales of the besetting ones in the garden of cruel roses, at that hour of shifting lights. Meanwhile, it was all too vague to speak of or actually complain about to our elders. For after all what was there to tell? He was always careful to remain at arm's length, soon fell behind, and taken at their face value, most of his remarks seemed inoffensive.

His interest in the local flora appeared to us as one of his milder, more human qualities, along with his kindness to animals, and so we never spoke of what, had Miss Pawley known it, would have caused her considerable concern.

The school was a curiously enclosed community, almost cloistered behind its inviolate front and elegantly draped lace-curtained windows. But for an occasional parent, one rarely saw a stranger on the premises, apart from the doctor if one of the boarders fell ill, or the retired Methodist minister who came once a year to give his annual talk on the work of the British and Foreign Bible Society. Only two of the teachers were Cornish: Miss Pawley and the mistress in charge of the Infants' class, who had been a former pupil at the school. All "lived in", and were never to be seen at public functions other than those directly connected with Pencarrow House, which included the school concert, the bazaar and chapel on Sundays. They took no part in local affairs, and oblivious to election fever during the campaign (when the school's handsome facade had remained as undecorated and non-committal as those of the banks and the municipal buildings nearby), our school mistresses were equally oblivious to what followed it, until made rudely aware of Pincher's existence by his unprecedented appearance one morning in the Upper Fourth classroom during a maths exam.

The first intimation that anything unusual was going on was the sound of the window blinds being drawn back sharply against the glass by a through-draught, caused by a sudden opening of the door at the foot of the stairs (the outer door having evidently been left open too). The next moment exam papers and sheets of foolscap were sent flying ceilingwards, where they clumsily circled before falling to the floor to blow about in all directions. Miss Merrick looked up from her desk at the front of the class and, unable to believe the evidence of her eyes, removed and carefully wiped her *pince-nez* before replacing them, the better to focus on an apparition slowly appearing through the floor at the back of the room. Like a pantomime demon, or maybe the real variety, came Pincher, carrying a coal sack, the acrid smell of which combined with a trail of black dust and the smudges on his person to make this idea almost feasible, especially for anyone who had never seen him before. Crimson in the face, he looked but recently come from stoking subterranean fires, a figure in black and red.

Miss Merrick reached the top of the stairs before Pincher did and though a small lady, from that position towered above him. His unlikely explanation was that having heard that the school was in urgent need of fuel he had brought some and was looking for somewhere to put it. And on Miss Merrick pointing out that he had actually passed the clearly marked coal shed on his way in, he said that he couldn't read. This may have been true, but the shed door always stood open, the nature of its contents obvious to passers-by. The voluminous folds of her gown, caught in the breeze which was now sweeping the place, spread like the dark wings of a mother-bird defending her young. She seemed about to fly at him and in his hasty backward descent before her he trod on his dog, which sent up a long-drawn-out howl.

Although on the premises for no more than a couple of minutes and having spoken but twice, he had contrived to create the maximum amount of disturbance, and it took some time to restore any sort of order, and the exam papers to their rightful owners. This time he must have realised that he had gone too far in attracting so much unwelcome attention to himself, and we saw him no more. He ceased to dog our steps and some time later he vanished from the town, having been sentenced, at Bodmin Assizes, to two years' hard-labour for some mysterious crime involving a small boy. At least, mysterious to us, for no details were given and it was simply referred to as "an incident" which had apparently taken place late one afternoon, somewhere on the waste ground beyond the cattle-market.

The end of term was always a pleasant time, especially the end of the summer term when, with the big exams over, many of the usual rules were relaxed. In December there was always the bazaar and during the week before Easter it was usual for the upper forms to put on a simple entertainment. This took place one afternoon in the large classroom in the annexe, to which the rest of the school was invited, and it was made up of songs, recitations, musical monologues and shadow-acting scenes contrived by means of a sheet stretched across one end of the room and illuminated by oil lamps from behind. This year for some reason it had not taken place and now, by way of a surprise for the staff and the other forms, it was decided to attempt something more ambitious: the Trial Scene from *The Merchant of Venice*, and to hire the Temperance Hall for the performance. The reason for the choice was twofold. First, as *The Merchant* was the work that had been set for the Junior Cambridge Exam the whole Upper School had been studying it and already knew many of the speeches by heart. And secondly, the platform in the hall was tiered above a wide open space containing a long narrow table and chairs which made it appear an ideal setting for a court scene.

The Temperance Hall had been built a hundred years earlier by the Total Abstinence Society because no one would allow it to hold meetings on any property, apart from the well-meaning hotel owner who rented them a room, so that the anomalous situation arose of people being persuaded to sign the pledge on licensed premises. Now the hall was used for public meetings and by the Literary and Scientific Institute for lantern lectures on Tuesday evenings. Each member of the Fifth and Upper Fourth contributed towards the hiring fee and the Head Girl, whose brain-child it was, made the necessary arrangements for the use of the hall from noon on the day before we broke up for the summer holidays.

At first it looked as though the costumes were going to be a problem, until a girl whose parents kept a drapery store came up with some unsold remnants of cotton material, and a variety of trimmings were found, in the way of braids, beads, fringes and cords left over from the July Sale, after which we were fully occupied feverishly pinning and tacking and sewing yards of gold and silver galloon on brightly coloured sateen. Then several unforeseen difficulties arose on the day itself. To start with, having relied too much on an over-all familiarity with the text, we were under-rehearsed and uncertain of our cues. Nor had we realised that although the tiers ensured that the Duke and Officers of the Court would all splendidly face the front of the stage, the characters arraigned before them would inevitably have to stand for part of the time with their backs towards the audience. Only Veronica, as Portia, arrived at a graceful solution and, while addressing the court at the same time managed to present an elegant profile to those seated behind her. Finally, not having had the opportunity to work out our moves on the stage itself, we tended to bump into the table and occasionally collided with each other. Entrances and exits were especially tricky, having to be made from one side of the platform only, via a narrow flight of stairs at the back and leading off to the room we were using as a dressing-room.

It was Joyce who held the whole thing together as the Duke, in a grey dressing-gown of decidedly masculine cut, fastened with police buttons, and in comparison to whom the rest of us appeared to be wearing too much glitter and much too much make-up, having forgotten that we would be appearing in daylight. Her grave, impartial air seemed just right for the part. She did not have to act, making lines such as, "How shalt thou hope for mercy, rendering none?" sound like her own thoughts as she turned an attentive gaze from one to another, imparting some sense of law-and-order to the scene and dominating it up to the moment of her final exit with the

Magnificoes and the words "Antonio, gratify this gentle-man, for, to my mind, you are much bound to him", which she addressed to a nubile figure wearing a man's shirt that had begun to split at the seams.

Fortunately, in spite of a few awkward moments when someone missed a cue or forgot her lines and had to be prompted, or collided with others on the stairs, it all went down very well with the indulgent audience, which applauded at every opportunity and, occupying the front rows of the hall that seated over two hundred, did its best to appear an enthusiastic full-house. Miss Pawley, who had dressed up for the occasion, was wearing a light summer coat and a black straw hat resembling a hanging basket of velvet flowers. She seemed pleased, obviously not so much by the quality of the production (scarcely by that!), but by what she called our praiseworthy initiative in attempting it at all, and the inventiveness displayed in the costumes. On the whole it had been a success and made a lively finish to the term, which ended next day.

CHAPTER
FIVE

Charlotte Brontë and a Move to Grammar School

Most of the boarders were weekly, going home after school on Friday and returning on Sunday evening, and for some time there had been only one boarder by the term, a farmer's daughter from Pelynt who, as she was on her own at the weekends, was allowed to have a friend to lunch and tea on Saturdays. Mary had invited me several times during the past year and I had immensely enjoyed these occasions (unmistakably social occasions although on the school premises), and the afternoon walk with a mistress followed by tea and toast on our own in the library. Now she had invited me to stay with her at Pelynt for a week in August.

It was no great distance, but it was the first time I had ever been away from home on my own. At Looe station the sight of Mary and her elder sister, who had come to meet me with the pony and jingle, marked the start of a venture into the unknown, which was enhanced by the brisk ring of hooves as the light, varnished trap moved off smartly. It seemed a long drive, deeper and deeper into the countryside and finally along a farm road that left the lanes and then continued to wander for some way through fields before reaching the farmhouse. At first sight, that house might have been the sole habitation in the middle of a remote island, for sloping fields surrounded it on every side, the long line of green meeting the sky everywhere, except only for the place, over a mile away, where Pelynt church tower rose strongly, a beacon against the blue.

Within, all was mellow, gleaming, and to my mind, "most awfully pretty". I had been given a bedroom in which the wallpaper was patterned with roses, realistically drawn with well-defined areas of light and shade resembling a live hedge through which indirect sunlight fell diffusely. Carpet, curtains, cushions, in fact almost everything in the room was in shades of rose, but for the green china basin and ewer on the marble-topped washstand. There were colour reproductions of Reynolds' *Age of Innocence* and *Angels' Heads*: a *Child's Portraits in Different Views*, as well as the framed religious texts in Gothic black type lettering with gilded capitals and brightly coloured borders, without which any bedroom at that time would have been considered incompletely furnished. There were three: *God is Love* over the bed and, above the fireplace, *The Lord is My Shepherd* and *Blessed are the Meek*.

It was a nice room to wake up in, as I did to cheerful sounds of a day that had already begun for everyone else in the house. Years before, as a small child waking early on summer mornings before it was time to get up, I had discovered that if I stared steadily at any object, picture, or pattern of wallpaper, I could, by then refocusing my gaze, make it appear detached and vibrant in the air before me, quite close to my eyes and radiating outwards into a phosphorescent streaming darkness. And although it was especially effective when the object itself possessed shine, like a glass candlestick or antimony box, really almost any little thing was sufficient to start it off. This faculty, which had deserted me as I had grown older, now quite unexpectedly returned with a pulsing splendour on my first morning at the farm and was to last for the duration of my stay.

As the days passed the initial impression of isolation did not lessen but, if anything, increased. It was rather like being at an outpost with pioneers or the survivors of an advance party. There was no telephone, and no sounds reached me from the outside world save, on Sunday mornings, for the pealing of bells from no fewer than four churches. No other human being approached the place but the postman, whom I never saw, as he came no further than the lane to leave letters in a box at the end of the farm road, whence they were picked up later by whoever had gone out on the milk round that morning, on his way back to the farm.

There came to be something rather exhilarating in this thought, at first daunting, of pioneers and survivors. And from the window of the rose bedroom I could see the church tower, one of two reassuring proofs of the continuing existence of a world beyond the encircling hills. The other was the exciting new invention I had read of but never heard: the wireless! In the handsome mahogany-and-red-plush parlour there was a crystal-set with two sets of earphones so that two people could listen at the same time. "Listening-in" gave a completely different sensation from that which was to come later, when with the advent of loudspeakers sound was poured into the surrounding air. And although meaningless in themselves, the constituents of some sort of light entertainment with songs and jokes, I was never to forget the first sounds I heard in this way. The careful adjusting of the earphones while watched by those around and the voice for my ear alone, the receiver of news from afar, meant that I could not take for granted the experience, which was rather splendid.

The family had been welcoming and were immensely kind and concerned that I should enjoy my stay, for ever asking me what I would like to do and eat. Unlike other mothers who usually had set baking days, Mary's mother baked every day. Her Cornish pasties were the best I ever tasted either then or since, and I liked to watch her making them at the long scrubbed table in the great kitchen. She always used quantities of parsley (of which there was a bed immediately outside the back door), not chopped, but generously in bunches as a fourth vegetable along with onion, potato and swede.

Then there were her blackberry pies, eaten with clotted cream. For it was the blackberry season and almost every afternoon we went blackberrying, of which I never tired. The smell of the fruit was the first hint of autumn, and the juice which stained our fingers and the bowls in which we collected the berries was the colour of autumn, or at least, along with the heather, one of the colours, quite as much as the russets and browns that would follow. Just as there was a fashionable shade of pink popularly known as "crushed strawberry", so now too there was this hazy mauve, "crushed blackberry'.

By the time that the visit was over the holidays were over, too, and the school reopened. I always liked the beginning of the autumn term, with its feeling of being the start of a new year, even more strong than at the real New Year that always came during the Christmas holidays, or the start of the summer term in spring when everyone's mind was on the coming exams. The re-arrangement of classes, the giving out of fresh textbooks and time-tables (guides to an unknown land presently to become familiar), the sound of footsteps in corridors and voices through open classroom doors, all interwoven with the strains of Handel, Mendelssohn and Mozart piano practice, reminiscent of the theme music from some continuous film performance, all made for the quickening of a sense of meaning and purpose, with so much at hand to put my mind to.

Looking back on it later, I always supposed Miss Merrick, who taught English, History, Botany and Needle-work, to have been the best teacher in the school. To me, she certainly made every class interesting, but this may have been because the subjects concerned were my favourites. The classes were most lively when the subject under discussion was not one of the set pieces, as *Marmion* had been, or the Shakespeare play chosen for the Cambridge exam that year, in which case all that was required was for one to commit certain passages to memory along with the relevant notes for the examination day, after which they might safely be forgotten. Miss Merrick was at her best when something sparked her off to talk with infectious enthusiasm on some point in which she herself was obviously especially interested, as when a reading from *Idylls of the King* led her to talk of the effect of landscape on certain writers.

She was quick to contrast Tennyson and Swinburne, who had both visited the North coast of Cornwall when planning their Arthurian works, with Hawker the poet-priest of Morwenstow, to whom the "Natural World was the dream of God", and whose *Quest of the Sangraal*, written in a little hut on the cliffs, far surpassed Tennyson's *Holy Grail* (as the latter was to freely acknowledge), springing as it did from the scene before him: "Heaven come down to sojourn on the sea". She suggested that in this he resembled Hardy, who years later was to write of the opal and the sapphire of that same sea, and of the "magic in my eyes" on his return from Lyonesse, in a series of poems that as well as being love poems were also the expression of an intense, an almost spiritual, response to the spirit of place. And of course, farther west there was the great sea rock, legendary scene of the apparition of an Archangel: St Michael's Mount, which had inspired such poets as Spencer and Drayton, Milton's "great vision of the guarded Mount" in *Lycidas*, and nearer home Sir Humphrey Davy, writing of the view of Mounts Bay from Gulval:

On the sea
the sunbeams tremble, and the purple light
Illumes the dark Bolerium, seat of storms.

Hawker had spent several years as a pupil at the old Liskeard Grammar School, and his name frequently cropped up if the subject under discussion happened to be poetry or religion. It was he who had reintroduced the ancient Harvest Thanksgiving into the church calendar, the fineness of the decorations for which always outshone those of the other big festivals, of Easter when fading spring flowers filled the aisles with the odour of corruption, and even the richly berried greenery of Christmas. For the superabundance of the harvest included not only wreaths and garlands but sheaves and cornucopias, and the smell of the grain and ripe fruit mingled with that of long-lasting dahlias and chrysanthemums.

As a Methodist Miss Merrick obviously deplored Hawker's attitude towards Methodism. A certain amount of religious intolerance was usual in his day, and to some extent in my own, but even so, his positive loathing of a teaching of which Coleridge, no less, had written in his copy of Southey's *Life of Wesley,* "either the Christian faith is what Wesley here describes, or there is no proper meaning in the word", appears to have been excessive. He had a special aversion to the idea of "conversion", which he considered a thinly-disguised form of sexual excitement and release, and to the concept of spiritual transformation being at times experienced physically, although as one familiar with the writings of many Catholic mystics, he must have known that this phenomenon was not confined to the followers of John Wesley. But as regards the implied orgiastic nature of conversion he may possibly have had a point; as a small child in the far west of Cornwall, I remember overhearing a certain stage of the Wesleyan Whitsun gatherings described as moving "straight from the chapel to the fields", and frequent references to "Whitsun babies", which puzzled me, as children thus referred to always appeared to have been born in January.

Obviously this was a line of thought that could not be touched on, much less pursued, in our classes with Miss Merrick, who confined herself to suggesting that had Hawker understood them better he would in fact have found much in common with the Wesleys' concept of joy as a divine aspect of creation and an attribute to God. It was a concept made much of in their hymnology in which, as she pointed out, the rapturous quality was something new, other hymn writers having dwelt more on Love, Peace and Rest, and less on this "Joy of heaven to earth come down" aspect, now expressed in such lines as

> Transformed by the ecstatic sight
> Our Souls o'erflow with pure delight.

Or, one of my own favourites,

> Hear him, ye deaf; his praise, ye dumb,
> Your loosened tongues employ;

Ye blind, behold your saviour come;
And leap, ye lame, for joy.

Hawker himself had somewhere described his own habit of kneeling or sitting with closed eyes and sending out a "Spiracle . . . from every pore. Gradually in such an atmosphere every fibre of the Soul brightens like gossamer . . . St Mary's silk . . . upon the grass, and becomes a Ray . . ." — *Spiracle*! According to the dictionary, an air-hole or blow-hole, or respiratory orifice for breathing in insects; and to me a splendid new word suggestive all at once of pinnacles and spires and auricles and miracles and space and a circling flight.

Although not Cornish by birth, Miss Merrick had been brought up in Cornwall and always showed a great loyalty towards the county. This was especially evident in some of her literary pronouncements; notably those relating to Matthew Arnold and the Brontës, all of whose genius apparently sprang mainly from Cornish ancestry on their mothers' side. In the case of Arnold (who, she pointed out, was a good Liberal as well as a good poet), "The Forsaken Merman" was more or less a variation on the theme of the Mermaid of Zennor, and essentially Celtic in conception. It was all there, that those who run might read: sand hills and sea stocks, a priest, a bell, a holy well, and a human lured from the church to the water by a creature of the deep. In the legend, a man; in Arnold's version, a girl who was to later to return to her kinsfolk on land. In both, the scene moved between altar and choir stalls and the sea depths: there was the same juxtaposition of sacred and profane, the same odour of saltiness and sanctity.

105

On the subject of the Brontës, Miss Merrick considered that while much had been made of the influence of Byron, *The Arabian Nights* and the Yorkshire moors, biographers had almost totally overlooked the Cornish connection in the shape of an inherited imagination tending towards the fabulous and preternatural, characteristically Cornish; and the influence during the most formative years of their lives of Aunt Branwell, the little lady from Penzance who, on the death of her sister, Mrs Brontë, gave up everything in order to come and look after the family at Haworth. Originally this had been on a temporary basis, but as the three ladies to whom Mr Brontë proposed in rapid succession after the death of his wife very understandably refused him, she was to remain for twenty-one years, during which she had retired to bed by nine o'clock every evening and was never seen outside the Parsonage save in church on Sundays. Perhaps only a fellow follower of Wesley's could fully enter into the feelings of this poor lady with her exhaustive collection of *Methodist Magazines* and lustre teapot inscribed with the words, "To me to live is Christ", marooned in a Church of England clergyman's household in such a spot and such a climate after the cheerful social round and mild weather conditions to which she had been accustomed.

She is described by Mrs Gaskell as conscientious "but with the somewhat narrow ideas natural to one who had spent nearly all her life in the same place", and what a place! Mrs Gaskell, who had never been to Penzance, had derived her information about the town from a life of Sir Humphrey Davy written by his brother Dr Davy. In order to highlight the brilliance of a brother of whom Coleridge, no less, had said that had he not been the greatest chemist of his age he would have been the greatest poet, the author had greatly exaggerated the barbarous nature of the society from which he originally came; and in any case was not writing of conditions as he himself knew them, but from hearsay, of what they had been like when their mother was a child. So according to Mrs Gaskell, quoting Dr Davy, Miss Branwell's home town would have been one in which, although the climate enabled a subtropical flora to flourish outdoors all the year round, "there was only one carpet", the floors of the houses being sprinkled with sea sand. Dinner parties were unknown; and amongst the upper class, their wealth accumulated through smuggling and quickly dissipated through drinking, there was "little taste for literature, and still less for science".

In fact, as well as being a market town and a busy port for the export of ore from the surrounding tin and copper mines, Penzance at this time was a watering place with cultural activities in advance of most country towns of the day. There was a grammar school, circulating library, several ladies' book clubs, the later-to-be famous Penzance Library that was housed in the same building on the North Parade as the Royal Geological Society of Cornwall, and in addition the Assembly Rooms (with "blazing chandeliers") in constant use for balls, concerts, and scientific lectures, a town theatre, and no fewer than three Banks. As far back as 1724 Defoe had described it as "a place of good business, well built and prosperous. Here are also a good many families of gentlemen . . ."

Miss Branwell was to show considerable under-standing of the difficulties likely to arise for the daughters of the vicarage who, should they not marry, would find themselves homeless on their father's death.

By her forethought and patient economies she was able to save enough money to pay for Charlotte's and Emily's education in Brussels, promise financial backing for the school which the sisters planned to open (without which such an idea would have been out of the question), and finally, at her death, leave all three, as well as a niece in Cornwall, the sum of three hundred and fifty pounds each.

In *Jane Eyre*, the heroine describes the nurse Bessie who "fed our eager attention with passages of love and adventure taken from the old fairy tales and other ballads", and speaks of the memory of nursery tales returning in later years. These lines had always been associated with Tabitha Ackroyd, the elderly village woman who came to work at the Parsonage and who, Mrs Gaskell wrote, "no doubt had many a tale to tell of bygone days of the countryside". But Aunt Branwell, the children's constant companion, who according to Ellen Nussey talked much of her native Cornwall, would also have had tales to tell, passing on much folk-lore of myth and legend, which must have been meat and drink to her eager listeners, whose imaginations for ever fed on the fantastic.

Without Aunt Branwell there would have been no *Villette* and no *Professor*, and apparently no *Jane Eyre* either, for according to Miss Merrick, up to Jane's departure from Thornfield Hall, this famous novel contained all the elements of the West Penwith legend of "The Fairy Master". In this, a penniless girl, called Jenny, is hired by the master of a "noble mansion" to look after a child of mysterious parentage for "a year and a day", the sole condition of her employment being that she asks no questions about anything she may see or overhear and never attempts to enter a remote part of the house reached through a door at the end of a long, dark corridor, normally kept locked. By day she and the child and the housekeeper and the master himself (when he is not absent), appear to have the place to themselves but at night she is frequently wakened by strange and alarming noises coming from somewhere behind the locked door and realises that the other part of the house conceals some fearful thing. Soon in love with her master, who talks to her kindly, though for ever warning her against the dangers of prying, her jealousy is aroused by the sight of him in the company of several beautiful ladies who wear diamonds which shine like stars, and one of whom he appears to especially favour. Finally, on discovering the secret beyond the locked door she is compelled to leave, and the story ends with her alone at the crossroads on a lonely moor, not quite knowing how she comes to be there, or in which direction the "noble mansion" now lies; mounting a granite rock, she weeps for her lost master. The scene is of course very similar to that of Jane Eyre, set down by the coachman on the heath at evening, sorrowing for Mr Rochester by the stone pillar where four roads meet.

Jenny's days with the Fairy Master are said to have "passed like a dream": Jane says that life at Thornfield seems unreal, and "You, Sir, are the most phantom-like of all: you are a mere dream." Like the legendary master, Mr Rochester constantly warns Jane of the danger of curiosity, and in replying to her enquiry relating to some unusual aspect of his domestic arrangements, uses the words of the Fairy Master himself, promising to tell her at the end of "a year and a day". Needless to say, such comparisons, along with Miss Merrick's insistence that Mr Rochester was much more like a figure from folk-lore than a convincing portrait of an English country gentleman and that the novel was permeated by the spirit of this old Cornish droll, naturally gave rise to discussions that greatly enlivened our classes.

During the term I was once again to spend several Saturdays at the school with Mary, and as always much enjoyed the afternoon walks which, although not officially nature rambles became very much like them when Miss Merrick was with us and the operative word was "look". "Look Mary . . . Erma, look," as she drew our attention to things we might have otherwise missed, like the small snail, *Vitrea crystalina*, with beautiful shining shells that ornamented the reeds and purple spotted stems of hemlock by the streams on summer days. And I wondered why they were there, unless it was simply for ornament. Perhaps it was to escape birds who could more easily have picked them up from the ground, or as likely, Miss Merrick said, they climbed to keep cool, well away from the earth temperature. Too hot some days for human feet, it must have been unbearable to feel it for all their length.

In autumn there was the work of what we called "the spinning spider" everywhere, not like webs at all, but drapes and shawls of chiffon glistening in the shade where the dew saturating them would not dry for hours, unless you raised a web cautiously on the back of your hand and, that way, took the dew from it. Once we came on a large dense web: layer upon layer spun over a clump of leaves, the centre curiously pulled down, making it almost trumpet shaped; and on one of us touching it, the spider materialised from nowhere and quickly disappeared into the centre. It was the only time we saw this spider, *Agelena labyrinthica*. What wonderful names the creatures had.

There were a number of good walks within easy reach of the town. To my mind the best was along the road to St Cleer, a village on the edge of the moors with a holy well and a fine fifteenth-century church that had at one time belonged to the Knights Hospitallers, surrounded from late summer onwards by the purple and gold splendour of the heather and late flowering dwarf gorse known locally as Cornish fuzz. North of the village was mining country, for centuries "streamed" for tin and during the 1830s also to "cut rich" for copper. Then, whole families had come from the older mining areas in the far west of the county, and townships of hastily constructed two-roomed, earth-floored shacks had sprung up on the moor almost overnight. Transport in winter being difficult over steep, badly made roads, a tram-road was laid as far as the head of the Liskeard-

Looe canal at Moorswater, where it connected with a line extending to the copper-shipping wharves at Looe. At first consisting of lines for an eight-wheeled horse-drawn wagon carrying ore and granite from the moorland quarries and on the return journey coal, it was later replaced by a railway for locomotive haulage.

No fewer than twenty-five flourishing mines were developed in this area but, due to the large finds of copper abroad and the consequent fall in the world price, they were subsequently abandoned, all within a period of less than fifty years. Now no sign of this flourishing industry remained, but for the ruins of the surface workings, towers of silence against the sky, although the local people believed that more metal remained in the ground than had been taken out, and that in any case you could never be certain when a mine was finally worked out.

There was something strange and illusory in the sight of ruined engine-houses on the horizon, for their doorways and windows opened, not onto a darkness within, but directly onto the blue beyond, so that anyone entering appeared to walk straightaway into the sky: "Then let a way appear steps unto heaven'. I never saw a ruined engine-house on the skyline without thinking of these words which, after the coming of Wesley, the miners must often have sung in the darkness as they climbed the long ladders to the surface at the end of the day.

The first time that Mabel and I walked to St Cleer had been during our first spring at Liskeard. We had stopped to look at some especially fine willow catkins with showy gold anthers growing on the far side of the hedge at a spot where there was a sweet heady smell very like that of gorse flowers, though no gorse was to be seen. The hedge was not high but not all that low either: the catkins barely showed above it. Climbing for a closer look, hoping to reach the flowers and groping for a foothold, I realised that it was not a hedge at all but a stone wall over which brambles and other straggling plants had grown, almost completely hiding it: and I found myself looking not, as expected, at fields on a level with the road, but down at what, at first sight and coming on it so unexpectedly, appeared to be some sort of maze about thirty feet below, part of which led into a vast opening in the ground immediately below where we stood. Even Mabel, not easily surprised, was as puzzled as myself until we realised that we were standing on a bridge above an old mineral railway cutting.

On the far side of the wall a path at right-angles to the road ran down alongside a hedge and, following this downhill for about fifty yards, we came to an opening leading into the cutting itself. Here, between the steep banks rising on either side, the smell of the gorse seemed more tangible than scent, more like taste: the taste of honey in the comb; and in the shade where the sun had not penetrated, a drop of moisture had formed at the base of every flower; the bushes glittered as though after rain. Hartstongue ferns and lords-and-ladies furled up everywhere, bright green through a torn lace of withered bracken, and the track having been lifted, the ground was mossy and pleasant to walk on.

On Sunday afternoons while we still lived at Liskeard

we were often to return to this spot, the nature of which, as part of an abandoned mineral railway, though now fully and rationally explained, was to me at least never wholly to lose its mystery. In the legends the pixy-laiden were always taken by the "little people" down such green alleys on their journey to the underworld. And although I did not believe that this was one, I did not utterly disbelieve it either, because this was exactly what it looked like. Not in the least like a railway cutting, it was more like a green lane or drove road, difficult to associate with the hum of industry and the rattle of rolling stock. One had only to look, only believe the evidence of one's eyes, to induce the willing suspension of disbelief and a consequent belief in, and expectation of, the mysterious and extraordinary. In any case, it was really quite natural to believe in an underworld, as of course Cornish people had done for centuries before the eastern traders came, bringing their sky gods. And it was always intriguing to imagine the seen as part or precinct of the unseen, as when at first sight, as a small child, I had taken a viaduct to be but part of some vaster structure, high and fantastic, either ruined and so in the past, or just as likely, still to come.

I could hear the fall of a leaf in the silence which was only broken by the beat of a bird's wings, though no birds sang here; and the sound of voices, hooves, cartwheels, and the lowing of cattle reached me but faintly from the world above. This sense of solitude made me feel like an intruder, a trespasser, almost a thief. I was careful never to pick flowers here and once, seeing Mabel about to gather primroses, was astonished that she did not feel this too. Highly agitated, I attempted to stop her, nervously gabbling that it would be better to wait and pick some on the way home, where they grew among the graves in the old Quaker burial ground and were much larger, with longer stems. "Oh, no," she said, looking at me in some surprise, "they are finer here". And so of course they were, as were the first violets, and both much earlier than those elsewhere.

A variety of vetches flowered in this spot from early March onwards, starting with mauve bush vetch that by July had produced slender pods. These sprang open at a touch, scattering the seeds which, lustrous black, spiralled up on either side, making them look very much like a flight of fantastic flies. Next came a lilac and white variety, and a scattering of brilliant pink. The last, in July and August, was what even the flower books went out of their way to note as the most beautiful — the tufted vetch which in places grew up through other flowering plants, further adorning them. And as some of the plants were high on the banks one could see the vetch here as nowhere else, from below, and look up through the racemes of amazing purple-blue.

Although there was such a variety of flowers it was perhaps the trees that I noticed most in this scene so close to me, without distance, with no background of landscape, no horizon: just the leafy tapestry of the banks on either side rising towards a blue dome, across which small clouds cast moving shadows over the brilliant gorse below. Dogwood flourished in the shade on the lower slopes, its red stems becoming ever richer as the year advanced, blood-red with dark berries; then

115

there was the wayfaring tree whose green fruit turned from yellow to coral before ripening. October was a good month for colours: not only reds and russets but pinks and lilac. The leaves of the guelder rose were suffused with gold above hanging bunches of glassy berries. The otherwise dead-seeming brambles still retained a few ragged bronzed leaves that wagged about in little air-currents, uneatable berries with fermenting juice, and a few late flowers which the Cornish called brimble roses, white, pink and mauve. There was a pink I had seen once, in childhood, in the quartz called "rose"; I had never seen it since, till now in the petals of the brimble rose. It could not be copied, not matched or mixed in paint. For in both petal and jewel it held light as well as colour, and was translucent, like "the color that no man could understand" of the legendary altar stone taken by King Arthur from "the whelming flood" and handed by him (albeit reluctantly) to the saintly prince in return for the removal of a dragon. As it was obviously a small portable altar it may in reality have been made from this quartz. There was usually some basis of reality in these seemingly-fantastic descriptions.

Here the hazel grew to a considerable height. It was, I knew, a tree of myth, the water-diviner's magic wand and, up to the sixteenth century, used to "find" thieves. Harry Locke often spoke of the moorland people's belief that a breastband of hazel twigs (lambs' tails) would protect a horse from the night-riders, those little people given to stealing farm horses from the stables and riding them to the point of exhaustion, and of the connection between the tree and snakes; of the magician's ring

116

fashioned from hazel wood on which adders had breathed, and a charm beginning, "Underneath the hazelen mot (root), there's a braggaty worm with a speckled throat".

For the last journey the pixy-led were always blind-folded. But sightless, one would have known this place by the honeyed sweetness of the air and, from late summer onwards, by the almost ceaseless rustle and hiss of the ripe gorse pods splitting in the heat and scattering their seed. One would have known the place, but not the hour or the season, for in the gully mist lingered, twilight came early, and even the plants seemed to have been curiously deceived, those of autumn and spring often flowering at the same time. And from the bridge above one could look down through the topmost branches of the great sallow, glistening with silver buds and known locally as "palm" (being the palm of Palm Sunday), to violets and periwinkles in December. Standing so a few weeks later, both feet firmly planted in the upper world where it was winter still, we had sometimes ventured to pick a stem of the showery-gold catkins by now begin-ning to break, splendidly erect, from buds on the male tree. But, moist and sappy, they always resisted, scoring the hand and splitting into ragged green slivers.

After we moved to Saltash I only saw the cutting on Saturday walks with Mary, and rarely in winter, the three-mile walk to St Cleer Downs being considered more suitable for summer. It was a popular spot for picnics and blackberrying, and the Methodist Sunday school Tea Treats were always held there. From the school we usually took a roundabout route which would not involve retracing our steps on the way back. To the west of the town was High Wood, so called because it was a wood on a hill, giving its name, Highwood, to the whole district. This circular four miles was one of our most frequent winter walks, our way lying through a valley, over a ford where five lanes met, along and below part of the old mineral track, and finally home through the falling leaves and already fading light of the high woods. By this time, the delicious prospect of tea and toast by the library fire before us, we instinctively quickened our pace: "Come girls, don't linger; we mustn't be late".

After tea we played card games or Ludo, having first looked up any botanical specimens collected on our walk, in *Wild Flowers Shown to the Children*. The library also contained a recently published edition of Gerard's *Herball*, abridged and with an introduction by Marcus Woodward. Although it was not so easy to identify the flowers from the seventeenth-century woodcuts as from the colour plates in the other book, the arrangement of each plant under headings — The Description, The Place, The Time, and The Virtues, each lingered on with a wealth of detail and varied by the author's observations and asides in splendid Elizabethan prose — made it good reading. For instance, he wrote of a hawkweed, which he called Great Mouse-ears, "the stalks and leaves bee hoary and white, with silken mossiness in handling like silks, pleasant and faire in view . . . [and] . . . grow upon sandy banks and untoiled places that lie open to the aire" or wrote of a bindweed grown from seed: "But an ignorant weeder of my garden

118

plucked mine up, and cast it away in my absence, instead of a weed, by which mischance I am not able to write hereof so absolutely as I determined." Each page was enlivened by vivid touches relating to the varying hues, lustre or density of the colours described, which included "glistering blew", "swart green", "overworne ash . . . cleer and shining, like a shred of white sattin newly cut from the piece", "delayed purple", and "red purple . . . with certain white spots dasht within the flours."

There was a specially glowing account of borage, a plant which had seeded itself in some profusion in the Liskeard garden where the previous owner had sown it near the hives, in which position it was continuously beset by the bees, even a few in the early mornings before the flowers opened, droning softly and hopefully; very differently from their resonant buzzing later in the day. Gerard described it as having leaves "of a black or swart green colour: amongst which riseth up a stalke two cubits high . . . whereupon do grow gallant blew floures, composed of five leaves apiece; out of the middle of which grow forth blacke threds joined in the top, and pointed like a broch or pyramide." And he went on to extol its virtues among which, when added to salads, was one to "comfort the heart, to drive away sorrow, and increase the joy of the mind" while a "syrrup" made from the juice "adding thereto pouder of the bone of a Stag's heart [was] good against melancholy and the falling sicknesse". There was seemingly no end to the virtues of this easy-going little plant which, in addition, made "a mann merry and joyful: which thing also the old verse concerning Borage doth testifie:

Ego Borago gaudia semper ago — I Borage bring alwaies courage."

Among those works in the school library never allowed out on loan was a rare copy of the 1840 edition of John Wesley's *Primitive Physic*, listing a variety of cures used by him on his numerous journeys throughout the land, along with hints on prevention and diet, and setting down "cheap and safe and easy medicines, easily to be known, easy to be procured, and easy to be applied by plain unlettered men", which had evidently been considered to be effective, as the book had run into no less than thirty-six editions. Rather difficult to classify, it always got moved around on the shelves so that though one rarely looked for it, one quite frequently came on it. However, since the introduction of the *Herball* it was usually to be found alongside that volume, maybe because it was felt that Wesley's use of herbs placed it in a similar category.

It was not that the remedies recommended were purely herbal; by no means, although plants were used for a variety of cures, externally as well as internally, such as a necklace of nightshade to ease teething troubles, a solution of calamint for bathing leprous parts, and marigold flowers to be eaten daily to prevent the plague. For nervous complaints, veal, mutton, and chicken were prescribed, and vegetables were to be eaten but sparingly, "the most innocent being the French bean whilst young". Both coffee and tea were to be avoided at all costs and, needless to say, wine. Other remedies included corals in a bag made of catskin, roasted mouse, frog baked alive in an earthenware dish, the hair from the shoulder of a donkey of the opposite sex to the sufferer, the moisture from a white "new snail" pricked by a hawthorn spine at sunrise, mole's blood, seven spiders rolled in a ball, separate spiders rolled in "middling pills", freshly gathered slugs, four woodlice alive in a spoonful of jam, and powdered earthworms.

The reason for the work not being allowed out on loan was twofold. Firstly of course, its rarity; and secondly, according to Miss Merrick, her belief that it should be read only by those already familiar with the life and work of the writer; in other words, by good Methodists, as it might otherwise be misunderstood and consequently open to ridicule.

As the term neared its end the speeding up of activities connected with preparations for the annual bazaar increased, perhaps most noticeably in the Friday needlework class, where feverish efforts were also being made to finish off articles intended as Christmas presents. On other days of the week there were two three-quarters-of-an-hour periods after lunch, but on Fridays the entire afternoon was devoted to needlework, and there was no recess. There was a general relaxing of rules: some of the boarders loosened their tightly-plaited tresses, and we were allowed to talk. Those who went home for lunch returned rather earlier than on other days to collect work-boxes and baskets shaped like birds' nests from the cloakroom cupboard where they were kept; and the whole class assembled early. One of the concessions on hot days in summer was the partial lowering of the Venetian blinds which, when occasionally stirred by a current of air, sent bands of alternate light and shadow wavering over objects or, splaying, followed the form of an arm, a head, or a basket of rainbow silks. Almost a social occasion, it was much looked forward to. Also, the library was open for an hour during which books could be changed, and it was the time for the exchanging of Autograph Albums with favoured friends. Most of us had Birthday Books as well, but somehow they had never caught on in the same way as those little albums with gilt-edged pastel coloured leaves designed for the inscription of verses or, better still, drawings in coloured inks. No girl was without one, and certain lines tended to recur. In my own, "Be good, sweet maid, and let who will be clever . . . " no fewer than four times. "The rose is red, the violet blue . . ." was another favourite, inevitably surrounded by a flowery border.

As regards our needlework, we did more or less what we liked, working from transfers ironed off at home onto whatever article we intended decorating; a method that insured a considerable variety of table-centres, table-runners, chairbacks, cushion covers, and tea-cosies. And recently a new fashion had swept the Upper School: *camisoles*, which were regarded as decidedly sophisticated. Upon these we lavished much thought and careful stitching, and yards of ribbon and lace. They were completely shapeless, no concession being made to varying curves, and simply consisted of rectangular lengths of nainsook (a fine cotton with a silky finish), seamed at the sides, the lower edges hemmed to hold elastic, the upper decorated with lace threaded with ribbon, two more lengths of which were sewn on as shoulder straps. An additional decoration in the shape of an appliqué four-petalled Art Nouveau rose was optional, but was occasionally added on the left side, like a favour, above the heart. The écru lace edged with pale green leaves and pink, blue and yellow roses, was obtainable in a variety of widths from (and only from) a little fancy-goods shop in one of the lanes near the Pipe Well, which most of us patronised regularly. But I never remember anyone wearing one of these garments, which offered neither extra warmth nor support, but the fashioning of which gave us so much pleasure.

Unlike myself and most of the others, neither Joyce nor Veronica had succumbed to this craze, and they were both engaged in embroidering cushion covers. Veronica's was a seventeenth-century highly stylized design of honeysuckle from Popham's (the Plymouth equivalent of Harrods), worked in mellow crewel wools that would blend perfectly with the surroundings for which it was eventually destined. Joyce's cover was of "crash", an exceptionally strong mixture of jute and cotton, the making up of which was giving her some trouble, having to be done slowly and painstakingly, an inch at a time, as it was too stiff to go through a sewing machine. It was intended as a surprise for her mother, and would possibly outlast the Bayeux Tapestry, being wrought in a strong twisted mercerized thread more durable than

Veronica's fine wools or the stranded silks and cottons favoured by the rest of us. The scene depicted a cottage doorway opening onto a strip of crazy-paving which ran between well-kept herbaceous borders. The crazy-paving led past a dovecot, and along it a lady wearing a crinoline and a poke-bonnet so large that it completely obliterated her features cautiously advanced carrying a watering can. This nostalgic figure in its rural setting was very popular at the time, and was usually obtainable as a transfer, sold along with the necessary embroidery threads for working it, which were supplied by the enterprising manufacturer of both transfer and threads. Variations of the design were to appear on calendars, greeting cards and the covers of women's magazines throughout the whole of the decade. But characteristically, Joyce had contrived to make it unmistakably her own by the addition of extra birds and butterflies, a mass of little white clouds and a scattering of daisies: a garden for all seasons through which the gaze could wander from daffodils to dahlias.

Towards the end of afternoon school in winter the classroom was flooded by the level rays of the setting sun that filtered through the topmost branches of leafless trees in the gardens of neighbouring houses, sparkling in vibrant ever-shifting patterns on the walls, as if they shone through water. There was something in the air at that hour that gave one a feeling of hope and promise stronger and more robust than that of spring. Even the birds seemed to feel it, twittering at twilight, and breaking into little bursts and spurts of song, from late November onwards. Somehow these things always appeared more noticeable on Fridays, probably because on other days, intent on dates or grammar or equations, there was no time to pause and stare at floating lights and shadows that grew longer as the shortest day drew near.

Certain times in my life shine out like jewels set in silver: Angela Brazil at Polperro, the curtain rising on Neptune's palace, our walks through the falling leaves of the high woods in winter, the first glimpse of the mysterious green track leading one knew not where; and, such too were these Fridays. I think I expected them to last for ever; for ever and ever: did not think of the future or see the vista of the years. Only an eternal prospect of Fridays with things remaining as they always had been, as they would in Joyce's embroidered garden where the flowers would never wither nor the seasons pass.

One of the most pleasant aspects of those afternoons was being read aloud to from some work which, although encouraged to discuss, we were not compelled to study. As this class in the annexe was large, consisting of the Third Form, the Lower and Upper Fourth, and the Fifth Form, and included all ages from ten years to sixteen, considerable thought had to be given to the choice of reading matter: while mainly aimed at the older girls as those most likely to take an intelligent interest, it had also to be suited to the ears of ten-yearolds and as innocuous as the daily intake of the Children's Bible. This of course considerably limited the choice. Jane Austen was considered unsuitable, and so were the Brontës. Knowing it was about life in a girls' school we had once asked for *Villette* when the subject of the Brontës' Cornish heritage had cropped up in an English lesson, and had been refused. *Lorna Doone* had been followed by *Livingstone the Pathfinder* by Basil Matthews, each chapter of which was introduced by carefully selected passages from *Le Morte d'Arthur* or *Leaves of Grass*, enclosed within a heavy black border, like a mourning card. All but the last, that is, in which Livingstone's own words, "I go back to Africa to make an open path for commerce and Christianity; do you carry out the work which I have begun . . ." appeared alongside Whitman's "Pioneers! O Pioneers!" And we were now about half-way through *Mary Slessor of Calabar*.

Progress through any work tended to be slow, being subject to endless interruptions as girls came up for help or advice with their work. Sometimes quite a little queue formed alongside Miss Merrick who sat, not as at other times at the high desk facing the class, but in the middle of the room where a space had been cleared among the desks for a chair and small table. Though remembering few of the details of the story, I can still recall some of the chapter headings as well as the look of the faded, well-thumbed volume, as Miss Merrick paused in her reading to turn towards us a map of the Calabar Mission Field or a page of illustrations: "Miss Slessor's Heathen Friend Ma Eme", "The First Church in Okoyong", "King Eyo's State Canoe". I also remember an account of the mysterious Aros, a people whom the writer described as "intelligent and subtle . . . more intellectual and commercial than warlike", who had developed two lines of activity: trade and religion. They had "made one serve the other", their chief commodity being slaves, of whom they kept a plentiful supply at a creek situated in a closely-guarded secret gorge known as the Long Juju. When supplies ran short the mercenaries who were employed to capture the slaves had been known to slaughter and eat as many as sixty villagers during a single raid. Occasionally slaves were loaned out on approval, to be collected later on if not satisfactory. And regular slave-routes had been opened up throughout the surrounding country.

It all made interesting reading: as good as *Lorna Doone*, and in some ways similar. The Doone Valley with its closely guarded gateway which was not a gateway at all, but a barren darkness to go through between black rocks, every dwelling a house of murder, was not unlike the Long Juju. John Ridd, watching a cavalcade of Doones pass like clouds against a red sunset, one with a child flung over his saddle-bow, wondered if they intended to eat it. There was the same sense of lawlessness in both books, the same violence, even in some of the descriptions of the landscape: the horrific rending of the oaks in the Great Frost, the swollen waters of the moor coming down like a roan horse rearing at the leap of the hedges, the same dark places. Gathered around the alert little mistress in the room of ever-shifting light and shadow, there was something very intriguing in listening to these tales of savagery while embroidering thornless roses and threading ribbon through lace.

Descriptions of the bloodstained altars of Aros, the slaughter by the Doones of the inhabitants of an entire village (save for the solitary child left alive who had lost its reason) in revenge for the killing of one of their number, the mournsome sound made by the swinging chains of the sheep-stealer's gallows, were considered perfectly suited to the ears of all hearers, from the Third Form upwards. On the other hand, the entire school required to be shielded from certain aspects of *Jane Eyre* and *Villette*, both of which Miss Merrick had dismissed as unsuitable for reading aloud, ostensibly on the grounds that they were "unrealistic". Perhaps at heart she was averse to the idea of passion as having any place in the life of a respectable single woman, and especially that of a school mistress.

It was at the close of one of these Friday afternoon classes towards the end of term that a curious episode occurred, isolated and unexpected and at the time, to me at least, inexplicable. The lesson was over and the lower forms gone to collect their satchels from their own rooms before going home. Joyce and myself, along with two or three others had taken our work-baskets to the cloakroom cupboard where they were kept, and on our return to the classroom found Miss Pawley there. She was talking to a group of Seniors and several of our own class who had not yet tidied their work away, in a low voice very unlike her usual tone of command that was conducive to attention in almost the full military sense of the word. It was unusual to see her during school hours not wearing her gown, and with hands that usually held books or papers moving restlessly over a desktop amongst a scattering of embroidery wools as she talked rapidly, but with pauses as though short of breath, on a matter which appeared to be of such urgency that I

128

wondered why it had not been announced at Prayers that morning instead of being left till so late in the day, like an afterthought.

Miss Merrick had moved to a window and seemed to be listening to a little bird in the garden below that had just started up a dulcet repetition of three quavering notes, followed by four, and then a wonderfully silvery variation on seven, and scarcely at all to what Miss Pawley was saying. This concerned girls who had to cycle into Liskeard from surrounding hamlets and moorland villages, as well as those who lived in the country just beyond the town itself and had a considerable distance to walk each day after school; for the remainder of the term and up until the days lengthened in the spring such girls would, it seemed, be allowed to leave twenty minutes earlier than the rest of us to enable them to reach home before dark.

Miss Pawley was emphasising the necessity of getting there as quickly as possible: "Do not loiter, girls, never loiter; never linger . . . never dawdle . . ." almost fumbling for words, when the door leading to the cloakroom opened and several Third Formers wearing their outdoor clothes surged through on their way to the staircase exit. At this she took a step forward and lowering her voice still farther, almost to a whisper, said "I am not able to explain all this to you with younger ones present. But one day you will know of what I am speaking. One day you will understand. Meanwhile always walk quickly in lonely places, at twilight, if you walk alone. Never linger, never delay. Please," she said almost beseechingly, "my dears." And then, clasping both hands together, she quite simply fled from the room.

Miss Pawley agitated, hesitant, and at a loss for words, Miss Merrick apparently not listening to what she said, and both obviously embarrassed, was something quite new. And strange as both the words and the manner of their delivery had been, their reception was almost equally strange. Silence fell when the Headmistress had gone, several of the girls flushed; swiftly exchanged glances were as swiftly averted. Joyce, to whom I applied for an explanation later, on our way to the station, asking her what Miss Pawley had been talking about, was on this occasion no help, brushing the question aside as of no importance and quickly changing the subject.

I remembered Harry Locke speaking of the travelling fairs at which, as children, they had always been told to stay together and never wander off alone for fear of being "fetched" by the show-folk and consequently never seen again; and of the warning, "beware of the Cheap Jacks, beware of the conjurers". (Jenny's greatest fear in one version of the Fairy Master was that she might have unwittingly strayed among such people). But there was no fair in the district now. And had Miss Pawley said "never speak to strangers" it would not have made much sense either, as there were virtually none. Everyone locally knew everyone else, if not personally at least by sight, and where they lived and worked.

The words were, incidentally, the same as Miss Merrick's in the wood: "Don't linger, girls, you mustn't be late", which had meant no more than late for Gerard and tea by the library fire, late for Ludo. But this recent

130

injunction was obviously in a very different category. Pincher's cruel garden came to mind and the thorny wounds he had spoken of whence later the muryans would be born, the unwanted, the strangers. Perhaps this calamitous accost to which Miss Pawley would give no name was of the same nature. Or again, there was the legendary *bucca-dhu* (black spirit), who haunted solitary places and misled travellers after dark, although as she was a staunch Methodist one would have scarcely expected her to believe in this figure. We were never to know if the alarm had been caused by a threat directly involving the "young ladies", as the matter was never again openly referred to, although for the remainder of the term the daily departure of about half the class at ten minutes past four instead of at half-past was a constant and slightly disquieting reminder.

One afternoon during the last week of term Miss Pawley sent for me. Descending the stairs to the hall I naturally wondered as to the reason, for girls were rarely summoned except for some serious breach of rules. Stairs and hall were thickly carpeted, muffling the sound of my footsteps, remote from the classrooms, and silent but for the ticking of the grandfather clock that was chiming the half-hour as I knocked at the study door.

The room was a combined study and sitting-room, with a desk near the window and plush-covered easy-chairs on either side of the fireplace, above which a large colour reproduction of Millais' *Ophelia* hung below a pair of elephant tusks. Miss Pawley's brother had lived in India for a number of years, not as one

131

might have supposed as a big-game hunter, but as a missionary. There were Indian rugs on the floor and further oriental touches in the way of ivory and brass ornaments on side-tables and on the mantelshelf. The predominating colour of the room immediately struck one as green, due partly to the variety of potted plants in green *jardinières* on bamboo stands arranged in front of the window, over which the lace curtains were usually carefully drawn and across which the shadows of passers-by in the street outside momentarily fell, wavered, and were gone.

Miss Pawley was at her desk when I came in and had obviously been working on the end-of-term reports. She smiled when she saw me and appeared to be in an unusually gracious mood as she proceeded to talk of my "steady progress" in every subject other than French and Maths. In the light of this, she said, she would be writing to my mother about arrangements for me to have special coaching in both subjects during the following term, thus enabling me to take the Junior Cambridge Examination in the summer, which incidentally, coinciding with the time for the annual London trip, would make that leave-of-absence out of the question in future.

"But I wanted to have this talk with you first," she said kindly, "to see how you yourself felt about it all."

Oh, I felt delighted, for the prospect pleased me mightily. I knew that my mother could afford the coaching, and that although as far as was possible she ignored the fact that I was attending the school, never having wanted to send me to it in the first place, and I was never encouraged to talk about it at home, I had always had all the necessary equipment and books immediately they were required. I had only had to ask for them.

The desk was placed so that Miss Pawley was sitting with her back towards the window, through which an opening between the curtains allowed anyone facing in that direction a partial view of the road and a fleeting glimpse of the upper half of anything passing by, presenting an insubstantial shifting scene, as the apparently real wavered, turning to shadow on lace before dissolving. It was Market Day, with a lot going on, and the raised voices, the cries of animals and ring of hooves appeared oddly at variance with the book-lined shelves, sleeping Ophelia, and the figure of the Headmistress herself, a study in black and silver, in this room seemingly so remote from the cattle-ground and the world of men.

She went on to speak of how coaching sessions might best be arranged to fit in with the existing timetable without too much disruption, and as she did so appeared oblivious to a commotion which had arisen outside, where above the existing hubbub a new sound could be heard approaching; recurring like distant thunder, but more frequently than thunder, and vaguely familiar. I remembered then from the days when we were living in Liskeard that bulls on their way through the streets always went roped and with two, three, or sometimes even four men, and knew that one was coming now.

Having indicated that the interview was at an end Miss Pawley rose, and carefully selecting a pear from a bowl of fruit on the desk, handed it to me; just at that moment a herd of frightened sheep scattered in the path of a horse which, loose and with flying halter, bolted past from the lower end of the street where, beyond my range of vision, some creature appeared to have run amok. Almost immediately there was a sound of rending, the crash of shattering glass and, above the terrible animal trumpeting of pain and fear, shouts and the screams of women. Next instant the shadow of something horned and fearful, on the pavement outside the window, appeared across the curtains and then, in the space between, close to the pane, the gigantic head of a bull bleeding from cuts in which some crimsoning fragments of glass still remained. It was a strange sight: beyond the fine-looking woman, beyond the lace and aspidistras — the Minotaur.

He seemed bewildered, as though partly blinded by the blood running into his eyes, and stumbled and hesitated, his head turned towards us, as if for a moment he would have thrust his way in, away from men with sticks and ropes and iron bars. But only for a moment, and then he was off again, up the Parade past the ringed bull-stone by which for centuries in the past men had baited his kind. There, as bulls were never known to charge uphill, he would turn, not to the open country above the town, but down Tavern Hill to the labyrinth of lanes around the well; and perhaps at the very heart of it, at bay, confront his captors on the steps by the water where Pincher had once stood.

Somehow I got myself out of the room. Backing towards the door as from a royal presence and clutching my pear like a talisman, a token, the wonderful rounded weight of it soft and alive like flesh against the palms of my hands, I hurried upstairs as the hall clock struck four. My pear was too valuable to eat immediately, and I kept it for several days, only to find, on finally starting to pare it, that beneath the still lustrous skin it was in fact far gone. I remembered then how Harry had said that a pear was perfect for only half-an-hour, having until then been ripening and after that beginning to rot. I thought it must have been the half-hour while Miss Pawley talked.

At home I did not mention the momentous summons to the study but, noticing that my mother barely glanced at my report, thought it best to allow things to take their course, and for the time foresaw no real difficulties. When, however, Miss Pawley's letter arrived during breakfast on the first morning of the Christmas holidays, its effect was electric. Stung by what she took to be an implied criticism of herself in an inevitable reference to my lack of the necessary grounding in certain subjects, plus the veto on future trips to London in the middle of the summer term, my mother lost no time in writing to Miss Pawley announcing my immediate withdrawal from her establishment, because in the future I would be attending the Grammar School.

As was usual when, without warning, she embarked on some totally unpremeditated course of action, those around were swept along in a turbulent wake. Christmas was more or less ignored. The holidays were spent in a feverish round of activity, with hurriedly arranged interviews (there was an entrance exam to be taken) and the purchase of a new school uniform. The pale blue blouse and tie had to be replaced by what would now be called a tee-shirt, a collarless garment made of stockinet, which after a few washings tended to either shrink or stretch, according to the temperature of water used, eventually declining through a variety of fading hues to a pale reflection of its original colour. No two shirts ever appeared quite alike, save in the case of new girls, whose matching greens rendered them easily identifiable as new; at least for the first few weeks.

Coming from Pencarrow House with its small groups of ten or at most twelve girls to a mixed class of thirty, none of whom I knew and of which the majority was boys, was rather like being unexpectedly deported overnight, and inevitably it induced symptoms of culture shock; a phrase which had not yet been invented but would certainly have been applicable. Most of the pupils had been there since the age of nine or had come on from Council Schools at eleven. And it was unheard of for anyone over that age to arrive from a private school in the middle of the school year. The classes were large, the standard high. And the curriculum included Latin, in which those of my own age were doing Caesar.

Among the things I noticed most was the hurry and noise, from the first early-morning entry of the boys, like a cavalry charge down the hall for Assembly, after which bells rang, feet pounded, and glass-topped doors, made not with handles but to be pushed open, slammed behind those passing through them. Most of the teachers lived some distance from the school, which was right out in the country over half-a-mile from the town, and could be sighted hastening along the dusty white road on foot, as none possessed a car, no less than four times a day. Some of the younger masters hurried with lowered head and what almost looked like clenched fists, as if the very air impeded them. Perhaps it was this enforced haste that, once inside, sent them with barely a pause to fling off their coats and on their gowns, hurtling headlong down corridors, their wide winged sleeves streaming around them, like giant condors about to take flight.

In other circumstances I would probably have found the sound of racing feet, of voices from the playing fields below high windows (which, from where we sat, presented a wide view of sky and passing clouds and on late afternoons in winter the first scattering of pale stars), of choir practices in the high hall, the whole brisk purposeful hum, exhilarating. The atmosphere was friendly and in many respects a good deal more easy-going than at Miss Pawley's. There were fewer rules and consequently fewer punishable offences, and no detention or "keeping in" after school hours to write lines which, when rarely given, might be done at home.

But, stupefied by the unforeseen turn of events which had brought me here — where the race was to the swift and to them only, and among whom I could never hope to hold my own — I went around in a sort of daze, unable to shake off the thought that had I made less effort, or indeed none at all, I would still be enjoying the familiar Angela Brazil-like atmosphere of the classroom overlooking the sunken garden. And there was something supremely ironic in the knowledge that every effort on my part had been slowly but surely taking me farther from where I most wished to be. It was rather like

Alice, when in search of the Red Queen, being told by a rose to walk not towards her but in the opposite direction if she really hoped to reach her, and thinking it such nonsense, as of course one would. But apparently that was how things were in the real world, and I had not known about it until now, when it was too late.

So I muddled my uncertain way through days that in after years I found difficult to recall with any sort of clarity. Among them only certain isolated incidents stood out, like a Speech Day when speeches alternated with scenes from *Twelfth Night* and piano pieces, "*In Dulce Jubilo*", and "Go to the dreamless bed where grief reposes", and I watched, as it were from afar, those whose honour it was go up to receive their awards and their coveted handsomely-bound, gilt-edged prizes from the hands of Sir Arthur Quiller-Couch, most of them with a wonderfully unhurried grace, like jockeys who, slackening the reins at the last, were content finally to saunter home, to win by a length.

All this was to coincide with a period of sickness that, starting with headaches, nausea, and loss of appetite during the first term at the school, was to become an almost permanent state of sickness, lasting for practically the whole of my time there. School, train-journeys, church attendance, outings of any description, overshadowed by the fear of being sick, became painful endurance tests; and the summer trip to London was a nightmare. The city seemed to fester in the heat, and it seemed strange to me, not that I was sick, but that others were not.

138

As time passed I could scarcely imagine ever being well again. And then quite suddenly it ended. My mother, whose irrational aversion to the medical profession had prevented her doing so earlier, finally took me to a doctor. He diagnosed a stomach disorder brought on by nervous tension, caused probably by the sudden change of schools; and his pale, pleasant-tasting medicine helped me almost immediately, as did the prospect of starting at Plymouth School of Art in the autumn.

CHAPTER
SIX

Seasons at Saltash

Saltash, during the time that I was still at school in Liskeard, had seemed no more than a place to sleep in, but it now assumed a more interesting aspect. It was certainly very different from the towns where we had previously lived in Cornwall, Hayle and Liskeard; more like an island port, being surrounded by water on three sides. Originally owing its existence to its sheltered position above the estuary, at a spot where the river Tamar was sufficiently narrow to allow wayfarers to be ferried to and from the Devon side, it was throughout the centuries one of the few links with the rest of England; and as medieval towns tended to grow up around feudal castles it had always been closely linked with the fortress of Trematon, sited high above a wooded valley overlooking the Lynher, several miles to the west of the town.

Thought of by some historians as the original Tamari, the ancient Roman settlement mentioned by Antoninus, the town known as Villa d'Esse, Ashburgh (later prefixed by Salt, to denote its situation on the tidal salt river), Saltayshe or Esse Rock, fostered and protected by the Lords of Trematon Castle, developed as a community

140

and a flourishing port long before Plymouth. It was, according to the words of the old song ". . . a borough town." While Plymouth was "a furzy down" and at one time seat of the County Assizes.

It was during the sixteenth century that it reached its heyday when boats left its harbour for all parts of the thenknown world; three Spanish treasure ships anchored by Waterside were seized for their splendid cargo of silks, spices, indigo and ivory (ostensibly by way of revenge for the reported pillage and scuttling of English ships in foreign waters); Drake and Raleigh walked the steep narrow streets; and Drake married a local merchant's daughter.

Throughout the centuries tin and copper ore, lead (containing a considerable amount of silver), as well as arsenic and manganese mined in east Cornwall, was brought down the Tamar to be shipped from this, the busiest river port in the Westcountry; according to one historian, it bore ships of any burden, but its commercial importance was to end with the coming of the railway in 1855.

Now, despite its decline, the town wore an air of quiet respectability, due perhaps to the number of retired naval and army people who had chosen to settle in one or another of the early Victorian terraces, or among the villas whose gardens sloped down to the river, some of which were equipped with boathouses and private pebbly beaches. There were also a good many single ladies of private means; having been born well before the turn of the century and seen the men they might have married die in the war, these now devoted their days to church work and bridge-playing, their ranks periodically swept by some harmless hobby such as barbolla, stencilling or poker-work, the results of which came in useful for bazaars. The term spinster, still much in use, was the one most frequently applied when describing these ladies, as though denoting a profession or implying a misfortune, according to the outlook of the speaker. Gossip circulated around bridge-tables, at afternoon tea, and behind the discreetly-closed doors of the choir vestry on Friday afternoons, when a band of well-dressed women bearing baskets containing small brushes, tins of Brasso and bundles of soft rags, assembled to clean the seven-branch candlesticks and altar vases. This was an activity they always referred to as their "brass-rubbing" and after it they normally repaired to a small tea-shop in the main street, there to continue their interesting conversation, while at the same time enjoying an uninterrupted view of passers-by.

Crime was virtually unknown, unlike in the towns where we had lived farther west, where street brawls had ended, as often as not, on the road to Bodmin gaol. There was certainly no hour of the day or night at which one would have felt it unsafe to be out and about in Saltash, as on Saturday nights at Liskeard. It was impossible to imagine a bull at large in the streets, or even such a character as Pincher. For although there was a large number of unemployed dockyard workers and boat-builders at Waterside they tended mostly to stay there, congregating daily in silent groups overlooking the slipway to the ferry, and were rarely seen at the top end of the town.

In some ways it was less like a town in Cornwall than a residential suburb of Plymouth, to which the local trains ran every twenty minutes. And it was at a spot some miles away overlooking the wooded valley beyond the hilltop village of St Stephen's, that I first felt I had crossed the border into a land of flowers, mazy waterways, and ancient churches and castles. Here, at the head of Norden's "Salte Creeke of the Sea", the keep of Trematon Castle was visible above the trees and beyond, surrounded by water over a mile upstream, the towers of the daydream Castle of Ince rose from a wooded bank of the Lynher.

The road to St Stephen's was popular for afternoon walks on Sundays, when from miles around all and sundry, wearing their Sunday best, could be seen converging on the churchyard bearing flowers with which to dress the family graves.

It was also much favoured by courting couples and the recently-wed who, walking arm-in-arm, turned back at the village, rarely going farther into the valley, which was almost like another country.

It was beautiful; not striking one at first sight as typically Cornish, but more like a seventeenth-century French landscape painting with the castle on the summit above breaking the skyline, and everything below that blueness looking as if painted on a dark ground: trees, river, bridge, and winding road; streams, pools, fragments of ruined walls, and tortuous stony tracks like dry waterways leading off at varying levels. They also led inwards through the density of shadowy places, so that

143

WITH MAGIC IN MY EYES

the scene almost appeared to be hollowed out; all of which was very interesting and intriguing.

Beyond the village I rarely saw a stroller or a cyclist. The few people who were around lived there, and they blended so well with their surroundings as to appear partly invisible. Preoccupied and intent on their own business, they would reply courteously to any greeting, and sometimes watch one out of sight. Their dogs, usually of the greyhound type, watched by their side, but, unlike their masters, silently and indifferently.

There was a Methodist chapel at the foot of the castle hill, and a massive Sunday School building of granite pointed with red brick, which time and the salt air had weathered to a lustrous rose. From it on Sunday afternoons in summer the sound of a harmonium and the voices of children, amplified and faintly echoed by the surrounding hills, rose very sweetly: "He gave me eyes to see them, and lips that we might tell", as they enumerated a variety of blessings bright and beautiful: flowers, birds, river, sunlight, the tall trees in the greenwood, "the meadows where we play", in words that went well with the place and the season.

A rather fascinating aspect of the valley that led one on, expectant of fresh surprises, was that one often did not see things until they were reached. To start off with, the road from St Stephen's, which appeared to end at the stone bridge, not only continued beyond that point but divided, one way winding around the side of the hill up to the castle, the other running alongside the water where, through the trees, there was a view of mudbanks with channels between, along which swans floated upstream to Forder, where the villagers fed them. The water here was ever blue; deep steel blue, at all times, and the mudbanks not mud-coloured but opalescent, on cloudy days turning mackerel-mauve and silver.

Half a mile farther on, the road again branched, leading on the left towards Antony Passage at the mouth of the inlet and on the right northwards into the surrounding country. At Antony Passage there were the ruins of an ancient tidal mill and, beyond that, the remains of a quay, relic of the old-time transport on the Tamar, Lynher, and St Germans rivers that must have played an important part in the industrial life of the area. And here there must once have been a garden. St John's wort, buddleias, fuchsias, orange montbretia, and purple veronica grew along the slipway to the very edge of the water, and all with the crystalline lustre of plants that drink lime instead of dew.

It was a silent spot: no sound but grasshoppers, the occasional cry of a curlew and the faint lapping of small waves on the rocky shore, which iron deposit had turned all shades of ochre and burnt sienna. And somehow it also seemed to be a very ancient spot, a thousand miles distant from the town, and much older, for despite its history Saltash was now undoubtedly very much of the present.

It was the age of Rumba and "crooning", a word derived from a Dutch verb meaning to moan, and used to describe the gentle droning style of singing much enjoyed by the young but regarded by their elders as effete; of charabanc outings and At Homes; in spite of the growing popularity of the wireless, of "making one's own fun"; Evensong and the church bazaar; not yet an age of anxiety. Although it was the period later known as The Depression, with a National Government elected at a time of world-wide slump (America alone, the former symbol of prosperity, had fifteen million unemployed), the world of high politics seemed far away. And the activities of the new German Chancellor figured on cinema newsreels, "The Eyes and Ears of the World", as part of the light entertainment along with fashion parades and tennis.

People probably read *The Western Morning News* and the weekly Cornish papers more than they did the national dailies. And Germany's internal affairs would, for news value, have scarcely equalled the account of a murder trial at the County Assizes, especially when, in those days of hanging, the accused happened to be a woman.

Less dramatic, but almost equally absorbing were cases like that of a well-known lady writer of works with a strongly religious flavour who, compelled to withdraw publicly certain unfounded and slanderous statements she had made about the behaviour of the Abbot of Buckfast Abbey in the confessional, appeared in court wearing a costume richly embroidered with sequins.

Then there was the High Church vicar who, having introduced into his church without a faculty a number of ecclesiastical furnishings and ornaments that were subsequently declared illegal, found himself at the centre of a storm involving the Protestant Truth Society and those members of his congregation who disliked his "Popish practices". The problem went back as far as

1919 when the Bishop of the diocese, holding a public visitation, had condemned many of these Catholic practices.

At the time it had blown over but now, over ten years later, it blew up again, with protesters raiding the church to break or remove the offending ornaments, and attempting to drown the Mass with hymns like "Stand up, stand up for Jesus". Detailed reports of the law suits and consistory courts which followed were to appear in all the local papers as well as the columns of the *Western Morning News*, and finally, under the heading CROWBAR RAID ON CHURCH — VICAR HELD PRISONER, on the front page of a national daily.

The brisk social life of Saltash centred mainly around the church. As well as the Boy Scout and Girl Guide troops, and the Sunday School, there was a large Bible Class, what was known as the GFS (Girls' Friendly Society) for the older girls, a Young Mens' Club, Mothers' Union, ladies' Sanctuary Guild (of which the brass-rubbing group, known behind their backs as The Brazen Sisters, formed part), and a well-supported Operatic Society. All of which combined to provide occupation, amusement, and a variety of entertainment for all seasons. In winter there were whist drives, socials, the Christmas bazaar and amateur theatricals, not to mention entertainments in which tableaux based on well-known paintings such as *April Love*, *The Boyhood of Raleigh*, Rossetti's *Annunciation*, and similar works alternated with musical monologues, piano duets, "Scenes from Shakespeare", and demonstrations of handbell ringing.

But the really big event of the year was the annual July Fayre organised by the local élite to celebrate certain stirring happenings in the town's history. During the Fayre a procession of familiar figures, disguised in wire and bombast, surged up the main street singing "Greensleeves", after which they made for the cattle market, where a number of stalls and booths were always erected, often rather precariously, in and around the cattle pens and within a few yards of several large manure heaps.

Chosen for its size and accessibility on the outskirts of the town immediately above the railway station, the cattle market nevertheless seemed an odd setting for such a gathering. Drum farthingales swinging like bells swept up sawdust and straw, or trailed through the discoloured gutters that ran from the pens into open troughs at the lower end of the ground, as the crowd, smothered in velvet and brocade and hung about with chains, necklaces and ribbons, milled round against a background of concrete and corrugated iron. But in spite of these incongruities the Fayre was usually considered a success, attracted trainloads of trippers from Plymouth, and raised a nice sum of money towards church funds.

A prominent figure on these occasions was the well-off widow from whom my mother had bought our house. Mrs Behenna was descended from a long line of famous mariners, "Gentlemen of worshipful extraction for several descents but made more worshipful by their deeds", who had lent their name to an entire age as founders of the Elizabethan navy. On official documents like the title-deeds of the house, she still retained that name of glamour and gold, hyphenated along with her married name.

She herself never dressed up, probably feeling the goings-on tended to trivialise rather than celebrate a past which to her was ever present, and when confronted by no less than four Sir Walter Raleighs and multiple impersonations of her own ancestors, she looked like someone compelled to witness the antics of those not in their right minds. Yet her presence in violet-flowered voile was considered extremely desirable, not only on account of her position in the county, "a woman of family", but also for the amount of expensively priced trivia she always bought and could be relied upon to later donate for re-sale at the Christmas bazaar.

Her husband, a Plymouth business man, had died two years earlier and she now lived alone with her son Richard at Alma Villa, a handsome house situated immediately below the station and above the terrace (though completely hidden from it by a rose-trellis hedge), from the high windows and lawns of which there was a wide view of the estuary. She was still in what was known as "second mourning", dressing in pearly greys with touches of violet and a variety of mauves, all shades of which vastly became her. Like the most illustrious of her forebears, who had occasionally been mistaken for Sir Christopher Hatton, the best dressed man at court, she obviously liked rich materials and nice buttons. And she always wore the great jewel, an intaglio engraved with the family crest, a negro in bonds, granted as an augmentation to the family coat-of-arms in acknowledgment of an ancestor's victory over the

Moors in 1562. It was an unusual ornament for a woman. But Mrs Behenna was an unusual woman, and at times a rather difficult one (according to the evidence of those occasionally caught in the crossfire), which was perhaps not surprising in one who seemed slightly larger than life, resembling some great figure from literature or the past. Meeting her always seemed something quite out of the ordinary; rather like encountering the Great Queen herself, or unexpectedly running into Hamlet's mother after church.

Devoid of the air of patronage which characterised the attitude of other ladies of the parish towards those less fortunately placed than themselves she was, on the other hand, no respecter of persons, choosing as often as not to ignore her friends and peers, looking through, not at them, as she chatted to the roadmen, or paused to acknowledge some passer-by's "'Day to 'ee, Miz B'henna".

Being slightly lame, she sometimes walked with the help of a stick. It was a disability impossible to think of but as the result of some battle-wound acquired far off, perilously, and long ago. It was most noticeable on Sunday mornings in church when, a dynastic figure, she advanced slowly up the aisle to her pew, and it was as though with her came *Saviour* and *Jesus of Lubeck*, those great ships with beautiful names.

It was in church that one most often saw people, or that one first saw those whom one might come to know later, and with ample opportunity to study them at close range, like creatures temporarily trapped in another element, silent, at least as far as ordinary conversation was concerned, practically motionless and unable to escape: bees in amber, to be studied at one's pleasure. It was all very interesting: especially the hands, moving as gently as in a current, the men's occasionally touching a cuff-link or tie; the women's (carefully gloved), a lace jabot, loose ear-ring or strand of hair. All, finally, were clasped in prayer and then unclasped, those likely to have contributed more than the token threepenny-piece being shaken by the vicar on the way out.

Considerable thought was given to their "Sunday best" by a well-turned-out congregation, many of whom, especially on the Feast Days of Easter and Whitsun, looked more like wedding guests. New shoes, which had to match the rest of the outfit, were a bit of a problem as the unworn leather, when under pressure, was inclined to produce a discordant note varying between a screech and a high-pitched whistle, causing considerable embarrassment to the wearers when trodden up an otherwise silent aisle.

The parish church, which had originally served as a chapel-of-ease to the mother-church at St Stephen's, was what was known as "High".

The eleven o'clock service on Sunday morning was Mass (the same as at the church we had attended in Hayle, where it had been known as Sung Eucharist; a subtle difference of approach), during which bells rang, figures in brocaded vestments intoned, bowed, knelt and rose again while the congregation, mostly with tightly shut eyes, murmured private devotions, some exhaling the odour of the violet cachous sucked during the sermon. All of which left me to my own wandering thoughts and, with eyes wide open, to marking time.

151

We usually sat immediately behind Mrs Behenna and, sparked off by an occasional glimpse of the jewel, I would try to recall school history-of-exploration lessons in which references to the great family of ship-builders, sea-captains and heroes had regularly recurred, wishing I had at the time been more attentive and now trying to piece something together from half-remembered bits and pieces: the Battle of San Juan de Ulua . . . he whom the Spaniards called Guillen Acquines marching into Rio de la Racha at the head of his troops . . . the private flotilla riding the Sound like a small Armada, firing on seven armed Spanish ships which, entering the bay, had failed to lower their flag and strike topsails to the Queen's ships lying at their deepwater anchorage in the Cattewater, continuing to fire until the customary salutes had been made . . . fragmentary snatches of this and that.

It was odd how certain things stuck in the mind, like what Miss Merrick had said about Coleridge first coming on the idea of the star-dogged moon (a piece of sailors' lore), in the *Observations* of Mrs Behenna's ancestor's voyage into the South Seas, and a description of multi-coloured water-snakes which were later to be those watched by the Ancient Mariner within the shadow of the ship:

> Blue, glossy green and velvet black,
> They coiled and swam, and every track
> Was a flash of golden fire.

And the words of a letter written by one brother to another far away and long ago, and reassuringly, of their

152

freshly furbished boats ready to leave dry dock: ". . . the ships sit aground so strongly and are so staunch as if they were made of a whole tree . . . it is done by torch-lights and cressets, and in an extreme gale of wind, which consumes pitch, tallow, and furze abundantly . . . the *Hope*, and *Nonpareil* are both graved, tallowed and this tide into the road again . . ." A shipwright's words, very exact, stating facts; and so hopeful and strong, somehow memorable, not easily forgotten.

My mother, while conceding a certain grudging admiration for her, had inevitably tangled with Mrs Behenna over the price of our house, and thereafter whenever her name was mentioned lost no opportunity to introduce some totally irrelevant reference to slavery into the conversation, ignoring the fact that at the time of the ancestor's engagement in it, the slave trade was regarded as being no different from any other branch of business.

From the first, life at Saltash had been rather different from Hayle's and Liskeard's where, as unmistakable *furriners*, we had lived on the edge of the society around us, making few friends and undoubtedly several enemies. At Hayle our garden had been destroyed in a night and a window broken, and at Liskeard things had been a great deal worse; from both towns our departure had been precipitous. All of which was largely, if not wholly, due to my mother's high-handed attitude to everyone crossing her path.

At Saltash, on the other hand, we had at once appeared to fit in. Almost immediately after our moving callers had arrived who, if they found no one at home, left visiting-cards, soon to be followed by invitations to afternoon tea. All invitations carefully specified "afternoon tea", which was always at three-thirty (for this the three-tiered cake-stand was as essential a piece of furniture as the chairs to sit on), as distinct from "high tea", a more substantial sit-down meal at five o'clock.

For the first time that I could remember, we even got on quite well with our close neighbours; at least with those living immediately next door, a retired school-master and his wife. At first they were the only ones we really knew. But we soon got to know a number of others by sight, for we saw them almost daily passing the house, which was at the end of the row, near the most frequently used entrance from the road.

At the far end the cinder path ended in a flight of steep stone steps leading down to the lower end of the main street. Presenting a gloomy aspect in the perpetual shade beneath the railway arches and haunted by stray dogs from Waterside, they were rarely used. Neither end of the terrace was visible from the other, and anyone entering it for the first time would have imagined themselves in a *cul-de-sac*, "delightfully secluded", as the house agent had described it, or simply claustrophobic, according to one's outlook.

It certainly was out of the way. No tramps approached it, no pedlars with trays of trinkets and toys, no organ-grinders or door-to-door salesmen staggering under loads of carpeting; most probably because none of them realised it was there. Occasionally a representative of one of the well-known daily newspapers would materialise, knocking on front doors in an attempt to persuade the occupants to place a standing order for the *News Chronicle* or *Daily Express* with their newsagent; in return for such co-operation they would, in the fullness of time, also receive a splendidly bound edition of some work such as *Pickwick Papers* or *Ivanhoe*. Coming from Plymouth, they would have seen the terrace from the train and hopefully imagined it promising territory.

And regularly once a year the auto-harp men, Mr Rimmer and Mr Ray, also from Plymouth, would arrive by train. Wearing dark suits and bowler hats, they presented a faintly bizarre, almost surreal, appearance as, perspiring in the spring sunshine, they struck sweet sounding chords, not by way of entertainment, but in the hope of selling one of the little instruments.

Among the neighbours we had first noticed, because it would have been difficult not to, were the people who lived at the other end of the row, in the house at the top of the steps.

There were three of them: Fenton, the owner of a small drapery store, his wife, and his sister who was a dressmaker. They were not local people but had come to live in the town several years earlier and were well spoken of, especially Fenton himself on account of his devotion to his invalid wife, whom one never saw outside save when being wheeled along by him in her chair, or carried in his arms as he took her to or from it.

The strange malaise which had so curiously shrunk her had in no way impaired her looks, which were of the delicate Dresden china variety. Although as small as a child, for which from a distance she could easily be mistaken, she was, at close range, quite unlike one: more like a fragile image, having a weary grace, prematurely white hair elaborately dressed and, under heavy lids, eyes so blue one felt she must be looking at everything through coloured glass.

She was always very well dressed, by ordinary standards almost over-dressed or "dressed up", as though Fenton and his sister were using her as some kind of display figure for their goods and skills, trying out any fresh fabric or new line in trimmings on her. She was a little figure with a set smile and voice no louder than a whisper, unlike her husband who was a prominent member of both the local Operatic Society and the church choir. Whatever the reason for it, her finery obviously gave the poor soul little pleasure.

The local clergy did not visit the terrace, which was rather surprising at a time when parish visiting was considered an important part of pastoral duties: but it was understandable, at least in the case of Birkett the curate. He was an ex-army man in his thirties who had been badly wounded in the war and had recently taken Holy Orders, presumably because he had found no other profession open to one so heavily handicapped. Getting around slowly on crutches, constantly falling (on one painfully embarrassing occasion in the sanctuary, spilling the consecrated wine), he was difficult to help, being a large stout man. The impression he created was distinctly more "officer and gentleman" than priestly, but he was considered a good preacher, having a voice

156

that carried, as did his laugh, like the rattle of stones down a dry watercourse.

One rarely saw him save in church, or in the little Baby Austin he used for getting from his lodgings, which were some distance away in the house of the widow of a naval commander. She was a lady in her sixties, known to be devoted to him, and he referred to her affectionately as "Granny". The arrangement obviously suited them both, and they brushed along pleasantly, their peaceful routine unbroken but for visits from Birkett's mother, a formidable lady who ran a hat shop in Bath, whence she arrived every few months in order to keep an eye on things.

Doubting her son's judgement in such matters, she apparently feared that he might at any time be trapped into marrying some totally unsuitable girl; unsuitable, that is, from her point of view. She was for ever writing to the bishop regarding the possibility of his offering her son a living, in which case she herself could then move into the Vicarage or Rectory, thus saving him from the clutches of designing women applying for the post of housekeeper. Apart from this obsession she behaved normally, and as an amusing talker and keen bridge player was always well received whenever she chose to descend on the parish.

The violent disagreements over some small thing such as a rearrangement of the furniture or choice of new window curtains, which had always been liable to break out at any time between Mabel and my mother, whose uneasy relationship from as far back as I could remember had been more like that of strangers compelled to endure each other's company than that of mother and daughter, occurred less frequently after the move to Saltash; at least for a time. My mother enjoyed the proximity of Plymouth, with its numerous cinemas and the large stores which displayed a much wider range of stylish goods than those farther west, and often spent the afternoon there; usually on her own, as Mabel had unexpectedly launched into a round of church activities which took up most of her time: Sunday School teaching and the Sanctuary Guild, and because a vacancy had occurred among the Brazen Sisters, as an addition to their ranks.

Equally unexpectedly, she had started to write short stories, several of which had been accepted and published by the *Western Morning News*, and all of which I considered quite wonderful, marvelling at her inventiveness and secretly envious of her ability to create fascinating scenes around characters with names like Kestel Polgloon, who rode their mettlesome steeds across Dartmoor, flourished riding whips even when there was no horse within sight, were wrecked and subsequently rescued off some spot such as Land's End and finally danced till dawn beneath the blazing chandeliers of Penzance Assembly Rooms. They were scenes very different from those around her, and I thought that creating them must be like being able to fly. Although she herself claimed little literary merit for these works, brushing them aside as of no consequence, as "pot boilers", I think was the phrase, she obviously enjoyed writing them and appeared a good deal more content than I could ever remember her.

CHAPTER
SEVEN

Art School Days

Coming straight from a Grammar School to a School of Art, with no period of gradual transition between, was for me rather like entering a foreign country uncertain of its laws and layout; it could be described as a challenge, and certainly felt so. The first weeks at Pencarrow House had been heady, and this, entering a world beyond the classrooms and no longer in gym tunic and blazer, was even more so.

Even the start every morning was exhilarating, as the train slowly curved onto Brunel's great faintly-vibrating bridge over the wide river. So was the city itself, Hardy's "marble streeted town" in the clear white light, reminding me of how one Restoration poet had described it:

> The streets be pight of shindle-stone
> Doe glissen like the sky-a,
> The zhops ston ope and all yeare long
> I'se think a faire there bee-a.

For although the entire district suffered from rising unemployment due to cuts in public spending and the consequent dismissal of dockyard workers, almost to the extent of becoming a distressed area, with over ten thousand out of work (plans to use part of the naval dockyard for commercial shipbuilding or as a terminal for ocean liners having fallen through), one was not aware of this state of affairs when seeing well-dressed people hurrying about their daily business through busy streets, with naval uniforms and signs of maritime splendour, both past and present, wherever one looked.

The sea itself, of which one was always conscious, was nowhere visible from the town-centre and for a view of the Sound one had to climb one of the narrow streets lined with gift shops and boarding houses that led up to the Hoe, walking up, instead of over or down, to the coast as one did in other places. On this grass-covered "high place", as the guide books described it, reminders of war and the glory thereof in marble, bronze and stone had been placed at intervals along the grassy verge of the wide parade area, the statues all facing towards the sea. A bronze Britannia, Lion of War and Sir Francis Drake, as well as a number of lesser mortals looked out over the gulf of waters that was bounded to the west by the wooded cape of Mount Edgcumbe. This guarded the entrance to the Hamoaze, which had been coveted (understandably) by the Armada Admiral, the Duke of Medina Sidonia, who had been so affected by the sight "though but beholding it from a distance from the sea that he resolved it for his own". On the seaward slope below, the massive lighthouse, Smeaton's Tower, had been erected on the sward after being brought granite block by granite block from the Eddystone reef fourteen miles out, where the sea had undermined the rock on which it stood.

The entire scene, dominated from whatever direction one approached it by the towering upward thrust of the Naval Memorial column, appeared curiously without depth, as some huge backdrop to which the clearly cut shapes had been applied on a groundwork of sky and sea blues and then, where small groups of figures strolled or formed knots on the grass, scattered with confetti. This impression may have been largely due to the fact that I usually saw it during the lunch break, around noon, when the sun was directly overhead, although even the picture-postcard photographs all seemed to have been taken at an hour when neither statuary nor tower nor high memorial cast any shadows, and only some of the young trees appeared to spring from pools of shade immediately under them. At twilight it was very different; then the pale esplanade and sculptures, rising above and between the light of the city and the shifting lights from the sea, might well have served as the stage set for some heroic melodrama of vast proportions.

At the east end of the Hoe the imposing Citadel, built by Charles the Second with, it had always been thought, the intention of overawing the townspeople at least as much as any foreign invader, stood on a bluff high above the entrance to the Cattewater; on the ramparts as many cannon pointed in the direction of the city as towards the Channel. In order to erect this elaborate mass of masonry the King had demolished the old Fort, built at the instigation of Drake and an ancestor of Mrs Behenna's and largely with their money, as well as the ancient

161

chapel of St Catherine. And he had obliterated the wrestling figures of Trojan Cortineus and the giant Goemagot cut in the turf and carefully renewed since time immemorial.

Both Spencer and Michael Drayton mentioned this legendary fight, which Cortineus had won by flinging the giant into the Sound, Spencer speaking of

> the Hogh besprinkled with the gore
> Of mighty Goemagot.

Cortineus had cropped up in Norden's preamble to his *General Historie of the Duchie*, in which he had disputed the authenticity of the supposed derivation of the name of the county "from *Corineus Brutes* assistante and kinsman, of whome our autients have ever called it *Corinea*, and afterwards Cornwall".

An art student of the 1930s might, years later, be forgiven for feeling that she or he had in part helped to invent the style which afterwards came to be known as *art deco* (although we never called it that), evolved partly in reaction against the curvilineal *art nouveau*, whose involuted, convoluted forms appeared to our generation to be about to fade and wither as we looked. Even in its heyday the appeal of this highly eclectic type of design, limited to those who could afford it, had never been strong. Few ordinary people were in a position to either dress or decorate their homes in a style which, eroded by amateurism, was dismissed by those who considered that they knew what was what as "arty-crafty". It was followed by a geometric approach

162

influenced by cubism and the shapes of machinery, and the idea that function itself resulted in a measure of beauty.

Melting colours were replaced by orange, emerald, violet and cerise; forms reduced to their essentials. From the first this linear, highly stylized type of design had a much wider appeal than the sinuous *art nouveau* genre, and was amply apparent all around: in architecture (the two really rather splendid new picture palaces rising in the city); streamlined tubular steel furniture; inexpensive jewellery (copies in jeweller's paste of diamond and white gold designs from Paris selling in the jewellery departments of the large stores for around half-a-crown, the equivalent of today's twelve pence); in the design of everyday objects like wireless sets, floor coverings, lamp shades and the like; and in the crafts, with emphasis on functionalism: "suitability for purpose", rather than on the additional decoration which, wherever it did appear, seemed to have crystallized or evolved rather than been applied. The triangle was a popular motif, as were the square, lozenge, chevron (used to represent streaming tresses and the waves of the sea as well as the sun's rays), and rigidly segmented circle and half-circle. Our geometry sets, along with a copy of the recently re-issued *Geometry for Art Students* were as indispensable as pencils and paints.

Behind this trend was the hope for the first time of fusing art and the best in craft work with the needs of industry, in defence of which Herbert Read had written his *Art and Industry* though at the time it never appeared to us as a trend, a fashion, or even a particular style, but simply the way things were. It was rather satisfying "materiality"; exhilarating like the daily journey, like the clear light of the city. In it everything appeared connected and everything immensely mattered, with art not in a frame or a glass case just beyond reach, but inherent in everything around. It was felt literally "ever at hand" as fingers closed with equal satisfaction on a set-square or a pair of triangular "diamond" dress-clips. It was a lively, meaningful time for us, through the way we saw things, the way we were.

The Art School occupied part of the same large building at the foot of Tavistock Road as the Technical College, lying beyond green glass doors opening off to the right of the wide entrance hall. The Design School was on the ground floor and the Schools of Painting and Architecture upstairs, as was the large woodwork room, used on three evenings a week for woodwork classes and at other times by those wishing to work on their own. The high wide benches allowed considerably more elbow-room and space in which to spread oneself than the portable desks provided elsewhere in the school.

There was what would nowadays be called a picture-window: a sheer sheet of glass filling almost the entire end wall of this room and affording a panoramic view up Tavistock Road, down which all day long the trams clanged, sparks flashing from points and trolley-arms. As the lights went up on late afternoons in winter it looked very much like some high, beautiful picture, and it always came as a surprise on entering the room from the subdued light of the corridor, especially when it was raining. Then it appeared an animated Monet, on whose streaming brightness the room and we ourselves, vaporous and insubstantial, appeared reflected above the scene of mist and fire below.

The standard of the school, which had produced Cecil Collins and Peter Goffin, was high, as was the pressure on full-time students working for one or another of the Board of Education exams. The attitude of the Principal was summed up in his words to a new student who had rashly let slip some remark regarding the enjoyment derived from using pastels: "You are not here to enjoy yourself, but to learn to draw." He was for ever quoting Michelangelo on drawing as "the fountainhead and heart" of every kind of painting and design, without which it was impossible to produce good work. And so before all else, we had to learn to draw.

Life classes were compulsory, as was "plant-form", and lasted three hours, by the end of which time one was expected to have produced a reasonably well-finished pencil study. During these sessions no other method or medium was allowed. Line-and-wash was "out", as were pen-and-ink, and the use of pastels, crayons or chalks. But we had a painstaking teacher, and it was a discipline from which we were to benefit later, though at the time finding it extremely irksome. For no deviations from this method, no personal preference or "good ideas" of our own were tolerated for the first year, during which inevitably some fell by the way.

There was Silvie who was lame and, to start with, eager. On her first day she had arrived with a sheaf of pen-and-ink drawings illustrating "Thomas the Rhymer",

"Goblin Market", "La Belle Dame Sans Merci", and a number of other works. In her drawings much of the flora and fauna appeared to be partly human, while men appeared like trees, walking; figures whose powerful limbs branched like oaks and who grew a tangle of greenery for hair, some crowned with thorns, their flesh bearing a variety of fungi in place of jewels. The knight in "La Belle Dame" had only one eye and in the other, an empty socket; there was a crystal from which his tears ran down, forming a pool in which little fishes with hands for fins swam through a rippling reflection of ruinous tracery of tree branches. The style seemed to suit the subjects, revealing everywhere the devious and uncertain, and sometimes unexpectedly the maimed: a foot, cloven, about to take root in the ground; a hand with but three fingers and, in place of thumb, a thorny twig. An open mouth revealed, not a tongue, but a small reptile. In another face a wound gaped where the lips should have been.

All the illustrations were finely drawn with a mapping pen and grew from the centre outwards, more like pillow-lace or a spider's web than drawings, an impression partly induced by Silvies's method of working which was, without preliminary planning (the "spacing-out" insisted on by our teachers), to begin to draw in the middle of a sheet of paper and work outwards, keeping all the while more or less to a circle, until the entire surface was covered.

She would arrive last for the life class and slowly take the only seat left, the one avoided by the rest of us, being nearest to the door, from which position the view of the model was usually foreshortened, and there listlessly remain, as though stranded, for the duration of the lesson. One leg, unbent at the knee, stretched uncomfortably between the supports of the easel and the hand holding not her pen but a pencil, to her a useless thing, idle. She was to leave before the end of the year, having evidently been classed as unteachable from the first.

And then there was "Mart" (I never knew whether Martin was his Christian or surname), equally intractable from the Principal's point of view, although otherwise in a different category from poor Silvie. He was to remain for over two years, during which, although never missing a day, he rarely attended a class. Arriving early each morning, he would hastily sign the attendance register in the first classroom he came to, before making for the woodwork room or, when that happened to be occupied, any vacant area where he might hope to remain undisturbed for the remainder of the day.

The sole reason for his presence on the premises was that they afforded him easy access to the materials as well as the working conditions he required for making his three-dimensional linear designs, built up on sheets of hardboard in stiff paper and folding card and coloured with a mixture of housepaint and enamel in black and white, blue, red and silver. Impervious to disparagement and disapproval, he lavished a wealth of care on these works, each one of which took weeks and sometimes months to complete and which when finished defied classification in any category accepted within the rather rigid school curriculum.

Although firmly discouraged by the staff, Mart's fellow students were on the whole inclined to admire his maze-like patterns, which did something to the eyes so that they appeared to alter as one looked. It was as if they came alive and breathed, and they, not oneself, moved, changing colour and changing place. A pattern in black on a white ground would, without warning, become quite a different pattern in white on black and yet another in blue on silver, leaving an after-image to superimpose itself wherever one looked or, if one closed one's eyes thinking to disperse it, grow on the dark within the lids. It was really like a kind of game, an optical *solitaire*, for each one was so designed that, looked at from a certain angle, it was sometimes possible to clear the board of images and feel childishly pleased to have "won".

Mart's leave-taking, when it finally came, was sudden and unexpected. A local member of Parliament, Hore-Belisha, who was Minister of Transport at the time, having seen some of his work and considering the technique to have unusual possibilities if applied in the realm of road signs, offered him a job. An article describing it all appeared in the *Western Morning News*, along with a photograph of Mart surrounded by his designs, and he departed in a blaze of begrudged glory for his own office at the Ministry of Transport.

Having at heart, I suppose, hoped to become a designer ever since the moment I saw the curtain rise on the shimmer and the silver of Neptune's Palace, I started off in the Design School, which covered a variety of

168

subjects: Calligraphy, Lithography, Dress Design, Embroidery and Fabric Printing, as well as a number of crafts. Among these the Industrial Design Diploma Course (so called purely as a concession to current trends of thought, having no connection whatever with industry, being the equivalent of today's National Diploma), offered far and away the widest scope, especially to those specialising in Embroidery, which was treated not as a craft but an art-form of considerable flexibility.

There had recently been an exhibition of contemporary embroideries at the Victoria and Albert Museum, contemporary not only in the sense that their creators were still alive but in that, unmistakably of the day and age, they could have been produced in no other. It had been permanently recorded in a book entitled *Modern Embroidery*, lavishly illustrated and with an introduction by Mary Hogarth, well known for her opposition to the tyranny of past conventions and the copying of work of earlier periods, notably the Jacobean, as popularized in the pages of the monthly needlework magazines.

This coincided with the Board of Education's appointment of a new examiner for the Diploma Course in Embroidery, the brilliant Rebecca Crompton, whose approach to the subject constituted a complete breakthrough. The materials she used in her own work had previously been unheard of as relating to embroidery: mirror glass, short lengths of ribbon, braid, piping cord, little pearl buttons; at first sight more like hastily assembled trivia from a dressmaker's work-table. Simplified shapes cut from scraps of organdie, "art" silk, tarlatan, gauze, were applied to backgrounds using a variety of different stitches and threads. The results of this direct cutting into colours and textures tended to be unexpectedly rewarding and lively. Her "Creation of Flowers" appeared less to have been sewn than to have blossomed within the area of the frame at moonset under a frosty dawn and, in the scattering of broken mirror seen through gauze, in places still to retain the glassy haze of rime.

Needless to say such methods were, in some quarters, considered to be highly subversive and there was considerable opposition to Mrs Crompton within the Board of Education itself. Groups of teachers were known to walk out of her lectures in protest against her "free ideas". But she was to greatly influence a whole generation of students who, excited and stimulated by the imaginative approach, were to regard her *Modern Design in Embroidery* as a veritable book of revelation.

After the summer holidays, among the new students in September was one from Liskeard who had been in the same class as myself at the Grammar School. At the end of the second afternoon there, having overtaken me on the way to the station, he had dismounted from his bicycle and, offering to take the books and papers spilling from my already overflowing satchel on his carrier, had fallen into step beside me. I had been embarrassed but also rather flattered by his attention, which was to become a regular occurrence as the boy, whose name was Julian, lived in a house in Station Road, which meant that when school was over our ways inevitably coincided.

In class, where his occasionally straying attention would be recalled by some teacher's tolerant "Dreaming again, Trethowan", his behaviour had been otherwise exemplary. Tall and fair, with a slow deliberate way of speaking as though carefully choosing his words and with very good manners, entering the classroom or hall almost silently, in sharp contrast to the boisterous slamming in and out of the other boys, the only son of an adoring mother, he gave an immediate impression of being rather delicate. He was in fact debarred from gym and games on doctor's orders: forever catching cold, a chill, or 'flu, during the winter months he was frequently absent for whole weeks on end; but the most prolonged periods of convalescence, tending to coincide with the final weeks of the autumn term, were obviously not unconnected with the creation of elaborate decorations destined to transform the house in Station Road into what would resemble a series of stage sets, in preparation for a Christmas party. To this half the school would hope to be invited, there being no limit set to the amount of refreshment which might be consumed, obtainable all evening from a buffet-like construction smothered in paper roses.

Now, several years later, he seemed very much the same as on that first occasion, with the same easy-going falling into step, the same mannerisms, only a shade more marked, like the slightly restless clasping and unclasping of his hands after first having run them through his hair, and the habit of prefixing his remarks with the words: "And then, my dears, you wouldn't *believe* it . . . but the most *extraordinary* thing . . ."

rendering them instantly interesting, apparently confidential, and usually highly amusing. He soon became popular with the other students. One thing had changed for the better, his health having unexpectedly undergone a sudden, an almost dramatic improvement: he was rarely absent.

About this time Mabel, now under the pen-name of Trystan Pensilva, an editor having suggested the use of a male pseudonym, was enjoying considerable success with her writing. As well as having had several stories accepted by a new weekly magazine for women, she was now a regular contributor to the *Western Morning News* Summer and Christmas Annuals: illustrated brightly coloured periodicals containing a selection of seasonable articles, stories and verse of West country interest, and costing sixpence.

As soon as a story was finished it was posted to Miss Agatha Timmins, a professional typist whose name and address Mabel had got from an advertisement in *The Lady*: "Authors' Work Undertaken, MSS, Scripts, Theses. Terms by arrangement." Quite a brisk correspondence had sprung up between Mabel and this lady, only child of a nonconformist minister, who since the death of both parents had lived alone in a house much too large for her on the outskirts of Exeter. Having few friends she appeared, not surprisingly, to be rather lonely, writing frequent and somewhat lengthy letters, and Mabel devoted considerable time to the business of replying.

Although rarely revealing anything relating to a fresh plot or to work in progress, once a story was finished and

172

knowing how much I enjoyed them, Mabel would often let me see a typed script before sending it off to a publisher. One day, when I got back from Art School, she gave me one to read which had come from Exeter by the afternoon post, about half an hour earlier. She had been looking at it before I came in and had removed the paper-clips holding the sheets, which now lay on the table beside the foolscap-size envelope in which they had arrived, addressed as was most of the correspondence relating to Mabel's literary activities, to Trystan Pensilva, c/o Miss Mabel Flawes.

In sorting them out to read I found two page threes. One fitted in where it belonged, between pages two and four. The second, which bore no relation to the rest of the narrative, I took to be part of some other MS, being written in the first person in the form of a letter, obviously from a woman, pressing the recipient, in the warmest possible terms, for an early decision regarding a definite date for their much looked forward to, but apparently frequently postponed meeting. It added that although they had never previously met the writer anticipated little difficulty in recognising her "favourite author", having already formed a very clear picture of him in her mind's eye.

Only slowly did it dawn on me that this was in fact no fragment of MS, but a letter addressed to the writer of the stories and penned by Miss Timmins, who was evidently under the illusion that she was corresponding with a romantic Cornishman, Mr Pensilva, whom she obviously visualised as being very much like one of his own masterful heroes. It was a surprisingly naive

173

assumption on her part and a rather surprising deception on Mabel's. A more observant person might have noticed that Mr Pensilva's handwriting was distinctly feminine and the name itself scarcely credible, the archaic Trystan of which, according to historians, Tristran and Tristram were mediaeval corruptions, having long been out of use, and Pensilva not a surname at all but a Cornish place-name.

As Mabel was unaware that a page from the letter had been among the sheets she had left on the table for me, it was quite out of the question to make any reference to it. Although naturally wondering how such a strange misunderstanding would finally resolve itself, Miss Timmins obviously not being one to be fobbed off indefinitely, as it was really nothing to do with me and only by chance that I knew of it at all, I gave little thought to the matter until unexpectedly reminded of it about a week later.

It was a Saturday and Aileen, an Art School friend, had come over for the afternoon. Our plan was to walk out to Antony Passage before going on to The Haven (abode of Miss Penfound, of whom more later), where we were expected for tea. Usually Aileen came on one of the little local two-coach trains that ran between Plymouth Millbay and Saltash every twenty minutes and usually I met her, but she had today arrived by a long-distance train from Northroad on the main line. Because of this she was a little earlier than expected and since I was not at the station to meet her she came straight down to the house. As we were starting out together a few minutes later, and were about to turn into the road, a figure appeared at the far end of the terrace, having evidently just come up the steps. She was a tall lady dressed all in grey in the fashion of about ten years earlier, her hair hidden under a felt cloche, and she was wearing a fur necklet, the lengthy tail of which, flapping up and down off one shoulder, created an impression of combined eagerness and agitation as with sidelong strides, listing over towards the houses and away from the bank as though in a gale, she loped towards us.

I had never seen her before but on Aileen observing "That lady was on the train," I thought immediately that she must be the Diocesan Sunday Schools' Super- intedent, who was expected in Saltash that week. Mabel had mentioned she was likely to call, as part of a routine visit to several of the Sunday School teachers. At the station, instead of coming through the wicket gate leading onto the road which passed our end of the terrace, as Aileen had done, she must have crossed over to the exit on the up-platform on the town side and from there enquired the way. That would account for her delayed arrival on the scene via the longer way round and the steps leading up from the street.

The fact that she carried a small suitcase, indicating something more than an afternoon visit to the town, tended to confirm this explanation of her presence and purposeful approach, as did her opening words on reaching us: "I wonder if you can help me? Can you tell me which house is Miss Flawes'?" Having indicated that we were in fact standing immediately outside it and not wishing to appear rude by abruptly turning away, I added something to the effect that it was our house.

175

"... I live there too; Miss Flawes is my sister." She smiled then, most unexpectedly, her face, pale and devoid of any make-up, flushing slightly. "Ah," she said quickly, "then you must know Mr Pensilva!" Realising then who she was and totally lacking the aplomb necessary in such a situation, I hastily mumbled some non-committal rejoinder before hurrying after Aileen, who had walked on and was by now in the road.

On and off throughout the afternoon I kept wondering what was happening back at the house. Had Mabel been the first to confront her visitor she might have thought of some feasible explanation for Mr Pensilva's temporary absence or even final departure from the premises (I did not know how far she was prepared to go, having already gone so far), and so have got rid of her guest. But in all probability it would have been my mother, unaware of the situation, who opened the door. And it was just possible, though not at all probable, that the whole thing would be treated as a joke by those concerned, who at that very moment might be enjoying a hearty laugh at it all. But that seemed unlikely, the grey lady having not looked like one prone to mirth.

I was never to know what happened. For although when I got back in the evening I found that during the afternoon, rather ironically, the Sunday School Superintendent had unexpectedly materialised in the form of a middle-aged clergyman who had stayed for tea, no mention was made of there having been any other visitor. Letters from Exeter ceased after this; and as far as Miss Timmins was concerned the rest was silence. I

176

do not remember ever hearing her name again. She might never have existed.

It was very shortly after this that something totally unexpected happened. My mother had been born in the Orkneys and had continued to live there after she was married, up to the time of coming to England a few months before I was born. One morning at breakfst, thinking it might be of interest, I started to tell her and Mabel about a new student whose parents ran a small guest house in one of the alleys leading up to the Hoe. On the previous day she had been talking about her sailor brother being engaged to a girl from one of the Orkney Islands, South Ronaldsay, saying that after they were married this girl would be coming to live with her in-laws at Plymouth. The effect of this piece of apparently harmless information was to render its hearers momentarily immobile, as with cups in mid-air they looked at me as though unable to believe their ears. Then my mother said quickly, "You didn't tell her that our family came from the Orkneys?" In fact I had, but noticing her unexpected reaction, I tried to pass it off with a non-committal, "No, I don't think so". As no more was said, I thought I had probably imagined the looks of consternation.

That evening however, with an air of studied indifference most unlike her usual direct approach, my mother asked if I knew when young Trinniman was getting married. On my replying that from what his sister had said I thought the wedding was to be sometime in the autumn of the following year, she said nothing. Several days passed without further reference being made to the subject, but during that time a growing tension between my mother and Mabel, which seemed to have been sparked off by the mention of the islands, became increasingly obvious. Rarely addressing one another except when absolutely necessary, they appeared to be barely on speaking terms. And then one night the sound of their raised voices woke me, and although unable to hear what was actually being said, apart from a sharp cry from Mabel: "Only God knows how I've suffered all these years . . ." I realised that a furious row was going on in the room below.*

The following morning, again with an uncharacteristic air of apparent casualness, my mother announced that before the autumn of the following year, as soon as I had taken my final exams in May, we would be leaving Cornwall. She did not say "before the arrival of Trinniman's bride." She did not have to, it was so obvious. And it was very strange. But so in a way had our whole situation been from the first. I had never really thought about it before, having taken it for granted: but I thought about it now. Fourteen years earlier we had arrived unheralded at Hayle, after dark, stumbling almost furtively down a road edged with laurel, to hammer on the door of the first house we reached, to enquire as to the possibility of beds for the night. As the years had passed without any communication ever being received from the islands or reference made to any living relatives, I had assumed that my mother had probably

*Note on page 227

178

quarrelled with them all so did not wish to remain in touch. Perhaps the oddest part of all this had been no mention of the father of whom I knew nothing, not even if he was alive or dead, until one day in a Hayle bank, when I was about seven years old, I overheard my mother refer to "my late husband, William Flawes", while filling in some official-looking papers. This complete absence, not so much of the father himself, but of any image of him, had always seemed odd. It was almost unnatural, like having only one ear or eye, and an empty space where the other should have been. In other homes deceased husbands and fathers were constantly referred to against a background of prominently dis-played photographs, so that one even had some idea of what they had looked like.

They speak of those who suffer from the God-shaped void which aches until it is filled, and maybe this one was slightly similar. But only slightly, for certainly I had neither suffered nor ached. Only at times, thinking to fill this vacancy, I had cut a photograph of some public figure approximating to my idea of fatherhood from the pages of a newspaper or magazine, to be kept for a while. Isaac Foot's had been one, and the evangelical pacifist Bishop of Birmingham, Dr Barnes, had been another. It was warmly inscribed to myself in invisible ink, visible at times only to myself, and that but rarely, as I frequently forgot what was supposed to have been written. This had been when I was very young. Later I remembered having thought Joyce's policeman father rather splendid, sighted once from afar on the Parade at Liskeard, walking slowly towards the magistrates' court, a man in a Roman helmet, spreading around him even at that distance a reassuring air of safety and security. I had not seen his face, only imagined it. None of this had ever weighed on or struck me as being particularly strange until now, when I realised that my mother and sister were behaving like those on the run; and for a reason unknown, which the sooner I understood the better. For although it was unlikely that I should be able to do anything about it I would at least know what not to do. The present situation was due entirely to my unfortunate mention of the Orkneys, and in future I might be able to avoid an even worse blunder. Obviously no one was going to tell me anything; and in any case it was better to find out for myself than to be told, for then the telling would get all mixed up with the teller. Better to find out, worry out, and face up to the calamitous on my own, at least to start off with.

Whatever it was, it must have been serious to have given rise to such panic; and my mind sprang to a variety of bizarre conclusions, of which involvement in such crimes as embezzlement, fraud or larceny were the mildest. Accidental manslaughter appeared the most probable. Knowing my mother's unpredictable temper, I wondered if perhaps she might have pushed or even struck someone who had then fallen over and hit his, or her, head and so died. Mabel, too, possessed a smouldering intensity, liable to break out less frequently but unexpectedly. Once when I was small she had seized the rag doll with which I had been playing and, throwing it on the fire, had watched it burst and burn, with a look in her eyes I had never cared to recall. Of course, on

180

occasion she could be kind too, but from as far back as I could remember she would at times suddenly appear totally preoccupied, not hearing what was being said and tearing at and through me as though at some far from pleasant scene on the far side of what was actually there.*

Perhaps she or my mother had unintentionally caused my father's death. Or, alternatively, that event could have taken place in a prison to which he had been committed for some crime involving debts for which his unfortunate family would be held responsible, could they be found. Any one of these explanations would account for the inexorable silence surrounding the figure of my father. It was perhaps understandable that these quickly reached conclusions were rather melodramatic, for so, after all, were cries in the night, the flight before the face of an unknown Orcadian bride, and the atmosphere of acute unease pervading the house ever since the first mention of Trinninman's forthcoming marriage.

*Note on page 227

CHAPTER
EIGHT

Finding my Father

On a side table in the sitting-room there was a rosewood writing box in which a number of papers, old letters, news cuttings and the like were kept. It occurred to me that it might contain something likely to throw light on the present curious situation. I did not know quite what I hoped to find, but I had to start somewhere. An opportunity to look in it occurred sooner than expected, one Saturday when my mother had gone to Plymouth for the afternoon and Mabel was at a safe distance delivering copies of the monthly parish magazine to subscribers living at the other end of the town.

At first sight the box appeared unexpectedly small inside, containing nothing beyond a fire insurance policy and several bank letters, but while running fingers over the satiny wood, I realised that a narrow section near the back, bevelled to hold pens, when touched at one end rose at the other like a miniature seesaw, opening up a compartment underneath, in which there was a number of papers. Among them was my birth certificate, which I had never seen before (and on which the space where the name of the father should have appeared had been left blank) and William Flawes' death certificate, dated over three years earlier! I cannot remember which I came on first, only that at one moment I did not know and the next I did: the one thing I had never thought of, *a moral lapse*, to be concealed at all costs, at a time when any open flouting of the so-called moral standards of the day carried with it penalties and long-term disadvantages, that are difficult to imagine now, in a more permissive age.

Years earlier, at Hayle, there had been a tremendous scandal when the daughter of a local tradesman (and a church warden at that) had returned from a lengthy stay with relatives in the North of England, bringing with her an "adopted" child. I had been told not to smile at her or the baby if I saw them in the street, or look at her in church on Sundays. Our custom had been transferred elsewhere in order to avoid the embarrassing possibility of having to speak to her in the shop, thus creating an erroneous impression of condoning her behaviour.

In Scotland the Presbyterian Church held even more extreme views on the subject. Children born out of wedlock and even those within it, if they made their appearance during the first nine months after the marriage had taken place, were refused baptism; and the mother was arraigned before the Minister and a full gathering of the church elders, there to express suitable regret for her deplorable actions before she could hope for re-admittance to the congregation. Few women, would voluntarily choose to face such ostracism when it might be avoided. Such a situation amply accounted both for the flight from the North years earlier and the choice of Cornwall as the final destination, on account of its distance as the farthest point of the British Isles, and the present trepidation at the prospect of the arrival of the native of South Ronaldsay.

There were a number of photographs in the box; among them one of my mother and Mabel taken in a garden overlooking the sea on what, to judge from the figures' embroidered muslin dresses, parasols and leisurely air of having alighted like large butterflies among the flowers, looked as though it were a Sunday afternoon in summer. Mabel appeared to be about eighteen, very animated and pretty with long dark hair reaching below her waist. Both were smiling as they looked at the camera, or perhaps at the person holding it, whose shadow, falling partly on my mother's dress and partly on the surrounding grass, though broken where the outline wavered over ribbon and lace, was clearly discernible as that of a man in a soldier's uniform. Despite the smiles and light of summer there was something inexpressibly sad about these fading images, so strange it seemed to have that moment, and the moment after when they had moved together, spoken, smiled again, lost for ever. The click of the camera might as well have been a pistol shot, so totally had it cut them off.

Carefully folded around this photograph as though belonging with it, was a cutting taken from a Kirkwall newspaper dated June 29th, 1914, containing an account of the building of a new pier by the Royal Engineers at South Ronaldsay, showing a view of the partly finished construction and, inset with his name beneath it, a photograph of the officer in charge of the operation, a tall good-looking man whose age could have been anything between thirty-five and forty-five; it was rather difficult to tell.

The date, nine months before I had been born, was a lead. And I never for one moment doubted that this was my father, who had also taken the photograph in the garden. The thought that filled my mind to the exclusion of all else was that he might now still be alive and that he might be found. As a child I had been greatly intrigued by the stories of Theseus and of Galahad, archetypal searches for the true descent, each culminating in a meeting between apparent strangers whose actual relationship could scarcely have been closer, although only one would at that moment, face to face at last, fully recognise the other: Theseus, who chose to go overland, the long way round by the Isthmus, in order to deliver the King's realm from monsters, and when he saw his father, "knew not what to say for his heart was in his mouth", and Galahad's cry through the night to his father Lancelot who had welcomed him aboard his barge in the dark without knowing who he was: "Sir, you were the beginner of me in this world".

At that moment, without the faintest idea of how to set about it or where to start, I visualised it as a search of years. The last thing I expected was that the find was to be so simple and so soon.

All I had to go on to start with was a name and a shadow on the grass. At first it did seem somewhat like seeking a needle in a haystack. We would be going to

London for ten days or so in April. It could wait. The Imperial War Museum would surely have lists. My plans were of the vaguest nature. The British Legion existed, did it not, to give help and advice to the relatives of ex-servicemen, presumably of all ranks? On our arrival in London I promptly started on the Telephone Directory. Major Ernest Mathews, MC (RE retired). As to be expected of such a surname, there were well over a hundred of them. At last I found it, but with no less than three addresses, one in the outer suburbs. I supposed there must be also other directories of military personnel. I decided to try a short-cut and, with the greatest secrecy of course, I rang up the British Legion office in Eccleston Square.

And so in the end so simple . . . no wanderings, no perils, no deserts, thirst or danger. A phone call to the BL office asking for an interview with Major Mathews, a second confirming the appointment at the HQ of Mosley's British Union at ten o'clock on Monday morning, and the thing was done. It could scarcely have been better, making everything extraordinarily easy.

That Monday morning seemed an auspicious one, with a hint of sweetness even in the London air. It seemed little short of miraculous that by boarding a bus or taking an underground train and walking a few yards I could be immediately brought into his presence. And so I arrived. Presently I knew that someone had come up the steps from outside; someone, but for whom I could never have walked the earth or seen the sun. No hurry, please let there be no hurry. For I knew that when he reached me I would almost certainly find nothing to say.

My eyes were doing funny things, his figure in a flux of light against a surrounding darkness, my heart swelling so quickly, so unexpectedly that it hurt, pressing against the flesh. There he stood looking at me. The human face, one of the most mysterious things on the planet. The human face, miraculous surface where the terrestrial light meets the light that lighteth everyman. The first sight of a wished-for face, the signs all written there but not yet understood.

He had of course no idea who I was; it was up to me to explain. I held out the photograph; it was the one of my mother that he had taken himself with his shadow on the grass. As I found words, somewhat falteringly, besides his being profoundly surprised there may have been a trace of embarrassment in his look, even a hint of suspicion, thinking perhaps that I might be going to ask for something or make a claim on him of some sort. Nothing could have been farther from my thoughts or intentions. When quite simply he asked me, "What is it you want?" I could but answer with equal simplicity, "Just to find you, see you, talk with you, get to know you a little."

Before too long this sense of my true intentions and simplicity of motive must have penetrated. For at last, "My dear child," he said. "You."

"Let's go out," he said presently, and together we went. From then on I was to feel and know that this man who was a stranger to me and so inevitably an enigma was indeed my father. We might have nothing in common except our blood relationship, but that could not have been closer.

"Where would you like to go?" he asked. "Anywhere, wherever you like."

"Shall we walk in Hyde Park?" I suggested, feeling that there we would be quite safe from any recognition of me. So there we went, his walk so light and swift for a man of his age.

The cause of my arising, but for whom I would not have walked the earth, he was unlike any of the men I had ever known; father-figures in clerical collars, a man in a Roman helmet. That had not been this reality.

"Things are not always as we would wish them to be," he remarked, referring, I took it, to the situation of our relationship. "And we must make the best of things as they are." I took it that we were doing that.

He was extremely kind, spoke to me kindly. I had never met anyone so alive. The way he looked at people, the way he spoke to people. And this life had given life to me; the thought was almost stupefying.

Girls and women always wore hats then; I had on a straw with black velvet ribbon and I knew it was right. Very thin straw. "How nice you look," he said.

I had nothing to lose, was more assured than usual. "Can we walk through the park and sit there till six?" I said. "Please. This once," I said. "If you do this I will go away and not come again. You will never see me again."

"Where you like," he replied. "Just wherever you like. Whatever you want. Yes," he said. "Yes, my dear."

That is how it was. But we met a number of times and this first was fairly typical of our meetings. Each time it was as though he had come from far away. The park was a good place, the weather amenable. He was a very good talker, making everything interesting and lively.

Amongst other things my engineer father was very keen on his plans for a Channel Tunnel, which were all expertly drawn out. I remember when he was showing and explaining them to me, sitting on seats in Kensington Gardens one day. It was a humid day. Vapour rose from the surface of the Round Pond. Suddenly a little freak breeze, ruffling the surface of the water, lifted the plans for the Channel Tunnel, carrying them towards the water. We both ran after them to the rescue.

My earlier thought of him, more as a hero than a father, was not without some foundation as it proved, for he had been through a grim time bridge-building and repairing during the hazardous Gallipoli Campaign in the 1914 war. (Was not Troy, too, a city of the Dardanelles . . . Hector, the gallant Trojan?) As he told me subsequently while we talked, comrades had been killed by shrapnel on either side of him. This experience had the effect of eventually converting him to a kind of Christian Science and the belief that his own life had been spared for some special purpose. He quoted, "A thousand shall fall beside thee and ten thousand at thy right hand, but it shall not come nigh thee," from the ninth psalm.

His detailed account of his own part in the Gallipoli Campaign was published subsequently as an article in an ex-services' journal, of which I obtained a copy. Though in it he treated the subject tersely in the forthright, factual and technical style of a responsible serving officer, I knew that for him there had been more to it.

There were passages that revealed incidentally the peril, daring, hardships, dreadful suffering, casualties and fatalities endured by those involved. Gen. Sir Ian Hamilton's *Gallipoli Diary*, John Masefield's *Gallipoli*, Henry Nevinson's *The Dardanelles Campaign* (an eye-witness account) are standard history and with Compton Mackenzie's *Gallipoli Memoirs* they all tell a tragic story, dealing at length with the disasters, muddles and mismanagements as well as the ghastly horrors, agonies and gross wastage of human sacrifice of that appalling, misconceived Campaign.

It was obvious as we talked that my father was concerned about serious things, the way the world was going, the seemingly dreadful drift towards war. Later, I believe, along with Sir Oswald Mosley, Gen. Sir Ian Hamilton and others, he visited Germany in an attempt to avert the 1939 outbreak of war. I do not know if my father met Hitler himself, though Sir Oswald and Sir Ian most likely did.

I wish I could recall now more clearly what we talked about and discussed at those momentous meetings we had, as we strolled side by side, perhaps by the Serpentine or through Kensington Gardens, or as we sat at table together. I could have been, I suppose, sometimes wrapped in a glowing haze of sheer satisfaction with at last having achieved, all on my own initiative, the object of my secret quest.

Naturally we discussed the Mosley movement, since this was his main preoccupation then. I did not fully understand it all and probably asked a lot of questions, even expressing doubts and possibly disapproval of some of it. But it did seem that these people were committed to trying to avert war, which to peace-loving, pacifist me (whose favourite father-surrogate had hitherto been the pacifist Dr Barnes) was the most dreadful of threats and horrors. (These trends in me, needless to say, my mother's belligerent temperament vehemently repudiated.) Some brave soldiers who have seen war at close quarters may well become the best advocate of peace. Though sharply aware in my own way of social and human problems, I was not perhaps politically-minded. The world of the Arts in all its aspects was personally, as in wider ways, my supreme interest, then as always since. How that would fare in a world of war, I may well have been wondering. My father's line, apart from Mosley politics, was of course professional engineering. His Channel Tunnel enthusiasms seemed in poor prospect of realisation in the international circumstances prevailing.

Still we met, strolled, talked of this and that. He showed some real interest in my current Art training. One subject definitely barred, as it soon appeared, was my mother. While scarcely expecting him to discuss their relationship of so long ago, I at least expected some acknowledgment of it. But as he turned aside any and every reference to my mother I soon realised he could not bring himself to speak her name. It was evident that their brief relationship had not ended amicably. He wished for certain reassurances as to my mother not knowing about our getting in touch and even then he did not name her, saying: "No one knows you have come?" He did not look like one ever in need of reassurance,

191

least of all from the likes of me, yet that reassurance he did ask for.

He usually stood me meals at Lyons Corner Houses. His gaze, even when he was looking at people who had just come in or were attracting the waitresses' attention, seemed to go beyond them, far beyond to battles and bridges and the country where the Turks had buried their dead among the flowers.

At any rate we made friends, with some genuine stirring of affection and hints of aroused gallantry on his part, between that so long unknown and wondered-about father and his admiring and gratified new-found daughter.

We said our final lingering goodbyes, with a last hug and kiss, he watching and waving a hand as I walked away, looking back at times until I could see him no more. And I thought and felt that these had been days I would remember all my life as though they were yesterday. Some events even while they are happening are already more like something remembered. And I felt that he, too, in the years to come might not forget me. Perhaps in his way he was indeed my Lancelot.

I never saw him again.

My begetting between my widowed mother and Ernest Mathews had of course occurred while he was stationed in the Orkneys in command of the pier-building operation there. It was while expecting me that my mother and sister felt obliged to flee from their disapproving Orcadian family and neighbours, taking refuge first in Edinburgh, then in York where I was born — hence my name as it was then, Erma York Chambers (my mother's maiden name), the somewhat unusual spelling of the name Erma being derived from the first syllables of my father's first name and surname. From York we moved for a time to a rather nice house in Scarborough; it was soon after the First World War shellings so places were going cheap. Then eventually by some strange choice to Liverpool, for too long a time, always it seems "on the run". Thence, to the great joy of small me, who had for so long scarcely seen a flower, we at last travelled south and settled in Hayle in Cornwall.

After that romantically secret meeting with my father while in London, on our return to Cornwall no correspondence between us ever took place. The episode remained mine and his, our secret. That is the nub of this extended story.

Revisiting Hayle briefly about this time recalled many vivid childhood memories, including a time when I had seen a local character Gale, (described at length in *A Grain of Sand*), legless as he was, rise up and using his still powerful arms grapple with a man he saw cruelly whipping and ill-treating a carthorse. The scene of the two men, one crippled, struggling together grotesquely, tossing and rolling on the ground while the horse reared and whinnied before bolting, was dramatically, gladiatorially, unforgettable.

Another much more pleasant memory was of the local signalman on the railway, who I fancy had a sneaking liking for Mabel, conducting her and me along the cinder path to take tea with him in the signal box; very unofficial and against regulations, no doubt, but not too difficult to arrange. What marvellous fun it was, between the sips of tea and bites of cake, to watch him have to go and pull over the great hand-levers so that the Cornish Riviera Express could presently go thundering, throbbing and whistle-screaming past.

Thereafter I spent my days as an Embroidery and Design student at Plymouth School of Art much as before, living in Saltash and daily taking one of the frequent local trains across the estuary from our Cornish side of the Tamar, crossed by Brunel's famous bridge, a bridge that would have been of enormous interest to my father. I met and made friends with some charming and talented fellow students, both girls and young men. Our girls' tea-parties in the studios and visits to each others' homes provided some happy memories. Among the young men, naturally interesting to me at that age, was Spike, who duly graduated to the Royal College, became a fine painter, especially I think of portraits and, I fancy, a most able Art Teacher too. There was Keith, a devoted young friend, who marked a page number and underlined a sentence in one of Chekhov's stories or plays. The sentence read, "If my life is ever of any use to you come and take it," but I did not come across his underlining until forty years later. Though he was a good sort and we got along well together, somehow I doubt if it would have been a success if we had married. Another pleasant young friend of those days and later was Douglas, who worked at a meteorological office, at whose home I was always made warmly welcome and who often took me to operas and plays at the handsome old Theatre Royal, since, alas, demolished although now rebuilt in a more modern form. Most of us also enjoyed going to the super-cinema, in large or small parties, to see the enthralling Garbo or Dietrich films. I sometimes cut life classes to do this, as they did not then interest me much. But I have not since found that these absences seriously affected my representation of the human figure. Studying the play of expression over Garbo's face may have been just as much use to me at the time. An older student, not really well known to me then, was Sidney Kerswill, a rather remote figure, as he was just finishing his last term at Plymouth before going to the Royal College of Art in London, to attain his ARCA. I spoke to him only once, briefly, asking to borrow some glue from the room where he was working alone, and receiving his silent, nodded assent. He seemed very grown-up and self-contained in those days. Many, many years later we got in touch again by correspondence, through his having been recommended to borrow *A Grain of Sand* by his local librarian and vaguely remembering me, jogged by Erma, the author's unusual first name. He was by then settled, more or less alone with his old dog Teddy, in a secluded Norfolk hamlet near Norwich, still occasionally doing a bit of the silversmith designing in which he had specialised. He had also designed and made gilded weather vanes resembling the drifter, the traditional local sailing boat, for Yarmouth Town Hall and another public building there.

A fine and most distinguished-looking older friend of those Saltash days was a gentleman everybody around referred to respectfully as Handsome, who I think was an architect, estate valuer or surveyor. I was envied for being seen in the company of this gallantly good-looking but married middle-aged man, who was fond of me in a courteous and considerate way. But I heard that well-meaning Mrs Bethenna, whose window overlooked Saltash station where Handsome and I would often await the arrival of the local train to Plymouth in the mornings, alighting together from an in-coming one in the evenings, had been known to say, "That little Hermia [as she always called me] had better be careful and mind what she's up to." As far as the ever-gentlemanly Handsome was concerned there was no need for her to worry. He took me out to some nice meals in pleasant restaurants and never exceeded a chaste and gentle goodbye kiss, from which, the first time, I nearly fainted with delight. It was also thrilling to wait on the platform and watch the majestic Great Western main line express steam in, knowing that it came from a greater distance than the little local train we usually travelled on together, on occasions when Handsome was on board and would presently step off it.

Quite another matter might have been, yet after all was not, my fond friendship with Neil, a mature young man met while he was visiting house-to-house in our part of Saltash, trying to get people interested in subscribing to the *News Chronicle*. He had great personal charm, was well educated and well read, introducing me to the books and writings of people such as D.H. Lawrence, Katherine Mansfield, Middleton Murry (whom I was to meet and get to know well long, long afterwards while acting as cook on his Community Farm in Norfolk during the war), and a variety of others. This opened a new outlook and new vistas to my intellectual, literary and aesthetic horizon.

Neil was always kind, gentle and considerate and never took any advantage of me. Nevertheless, it was discovered that he sometimes took drugs, had part-studied medicine, and knew methods for procuring abortions. All this seemed disturbing and doubt-inducing to those concerned about me. So, sadly and reluctantly, I was persuaded to end the friendship "in time". There might have been no real risk to me, but we could not be sure. I suppose he was of the species of charming and intelligent drifter, but he helped me a lot and I liked him greatly.

My two big experiences in love were yet to come.

CHAPTER
NINE

Canon Penfound's Daughter

A prominent figure among the Saltash Church of England élite was a Miss Penfound, a good-looking woman of rather uncertain age always referred to as "*Canon Penfound's daughter, you know*". As the deceased Canon had been a well-known hagiographer and authority on the lives of the Celtic saints the name carried considerable cachet. And then she was known to have studied at the Slade, and exhibited her work at the Plymouth Arts' Club exhibition at the Guildhall every November. She was also the chief instigator of the tableaux entertainments; herself a twilit pre-Raphaelite, a sultry if slightly ageing "Beata Beatrix".

I first saw her in church soon after we came to live in Saltash: tall, wearing a wide-brimmed hat and a cloak made of some handwoven fabric and looking interestingly remote. I little guessed then how I would last see her, with fine features so distorted as to be barely recognisable, and turned as towards one whose presence at that hour was an affront and betrayal. But that was all in the future. At the time she simply struck me as being attractive, and at once she proved to be friendly and agreeable. She lost no time in calling on my mother and Mabel, and it was mainly through her that the latter so quickly become involved in a brisk round of church activities.

Shortly after I started at the Art School she invited me and Aileen, a Dress Design student in the same year as myself, to tea. On this occasion she showed us some of her water-colours, charcoal and pastel drawings, and lent us a volume of Rossetti's poems. After that we were regularly invited to The Haven, one of a group of villas on the outskirts of the town bearing their names in Gothic lettering, in place of numbers, on their wrought-iron gates.

We much looked forward to our visits to the pretty house with its *art nouveau décor* and William Morris wallpapers, from which, moreover, we rarely emerged empty-handed. For our hostess was forever unearthing old copies of *The Studio*, interesting prints, scraps of some choice fabric, anything in fact of which she thought we might make use.

Gratified by our obvious pleasure, she seemed to enjoy our visits as much as we did, and when the long summer vacation came she arranged several sketching expeditions for our benefit. The Diploma Course included the History of Ornament and she suggested that we might find it more interesting to spend several hours making a careful study of one architectural feature *in situ* than to copy and memorise several from the pages of a book. She brought crayons and chalks as well as paints on these outings and encouraged us to work in line-and-wash. Although I suppose the standards of both were what would have been called academic, and obviously both valued excellence, her attitude towards the means of acquiring it was very nearly the opposite of the Principal's, for Miss Penfound placed enjoyment first, insisting that it was the first step towards doing anything well. There was certainly much that was enjoyable about these outings with their meaning and purpose, down echoing aisles, through stained-glass light and the soaring arches of castles, churches and chantries. Two of them, at this distant hour, still shine out like jewels embedded in the gold of summer.

One involved a church by a winding river: the old cathedral of Cornwall at St Germans, come on from above, through a churchyard where the strawberry tree *arbutus* grew. And within, every detail remembered: the granite-groined porch, the crockets of the canopy, the cusping of the arch, the Burne Jones window: the apostles all young and clean shaven; the knights without armour, the Grail at their feet, with the ferocious eagle, bull and lion harmless on their shoulders. The remainder of the window being clear glass, all the figures looked as if they stood among the trees outside in robes as blue as indigo (even some of the haloes were blue) and saffron and rose.

Then there was the wonder of Launceston: St Mary Magdalene's, built by the munificence of Henry Trecarrell after the death of his infant son and heir. There was half a mile of carving in the roof, over two hundred bench ends illustrating the psalm in which all things praise the Lord, and outside, the entire granite facing carved with angels and archangels, figures of Cornish saints, ferns and flowers all fair and fantastical in the sun.

Back at The Haven, after these delightful expeditions, there was usually tea, from exquisitely delicate translucent cups patterned with violets that made it taste extra good and with silver teaspoons shaped like flowers with long stems. There was always much to talk about, drawings to look at and those early editions of *The Studio* to spread out and leaf through after the tea things had been cleared away by the nice little maid.

Most of the better-off single ladies in the town employed what was known as a "help", usually a girl who had just left school and could be paid a very low wage on the grounds that she was being trained for good service later on, and also had all her food provided. Miss Penfound's help Bethany Trehaze, the daughter of an out-of-work boatmender, lived in, wore a black dress with a starched white cap and apron in the afternoons, and was always referred to as "my little maid". She was considered very fortunate to have found such a good home, indulgent mistress and comfortable kitchen to sit in on six nights of the week. On the seventh, her night off, Miss Penfound had arranged for her to attend the confirmation class which was held in the church vestry every Wednesday evening at seven. Removed from the perils and temptations of life at Waterside, Bethany really seemed to flourish and, well-fed for the first time in her life, was becoming quite plump and rosy.

The Confirmation was to be held on a Friday in July and two days earlier, on the Wednesday evening, there

201

was a final class and a simple rehearsal, during which it was decided where everyone was to sit and in what order the candidates would approach the chancel steps to kneel at the Bishop's feet. Bethany attended as usual but did not return to the house afterwards and several hours later was seen some miles from the town on the road to the creek; after that, she was never seen alive again. At first it was thought that she must have been going to meet someone and that perhaps they had both gone into the underground tunnel near the shore and been trapped, there having been several small landslides near the entrance recently. But when the passage was found to be empty the search was extended. And at the same time as the white-veiled figures were wavering uncertainly up the aisle towards the Bishop's footstool like a procession of so many child-brides, the waters of the creek were being dragged for Bethany. They did not find her then, and it was not until two weeks later that her body, monstrously swollen by the water and from which some of the flesh fell when it was raised, was washed up on the shore near the old quay. At the inquest it came out that she had been several months pregnant. "Foul play" was not suspected and she was buried quietly, almost furtively, in the cemetery on the edge of town.

For a short time it was as though, stupefied, everyone paused and then hurriedly went about their own business. It was best forgotten, or if that were not possible, best ignored. What had happened had happened and had been entirely the foolish girl's own fault. If anyone was in need of sympathy it was surely Canon Penfound's daughter, to whom the whole thing must have come in the nature of an affront after all her kindness to the girl. Life had to go on, and in any case it was now only a few days until the Fayre, the preparations for which were unusually elaborate this year. The church roof having been found to have death-watch beetle, it was hoped to raise a really substantial sum of money towards the Restoration Fund. Some of the men were growing beards for the occasion and many of the costumes were being hired from a firm of theatrical costumiers in Plymouth.

I had not been to The Haven since Bethany's disappearance, not liking to go there at a time of such sadness, and immediately after the inquest Miss Penfound had gone up to London for a few days, so I did not see her until I saw her at the Fayre. She was wearing a positively stunning costume copied from the "Armada" portrait of Queen Elizabeth, encrusted with pearls and bows of rose pink ribbon and, extremely flushed and almost girlishly fluttering a blue feather fan, was talking to the local doctor, Dr Challis, who looked very hand-some dressed as Sir Francis Drake and with whom she had evidently walked in the procession from the riverside. On seeing me she greeted me with her usual friendliness and said that I must come to see her soon and tell her all my news.

It was the hottest day of the summer, and it quickly developed into a series of minor disasters. Extra trains had been put on, the already-large crowd was reinforced every half hour by a fresh load of holiday makers from Plymouth, and the smell of humanity mingled with the stench coming from the troughs and steaming manure heaps of the market: it was as though just below the surface, under the fur and feathers, the imitation cloth-of-gold and "tastefully" decorated stalls, something tainted and sweating had stirred, and was now oozing down the soiled gutters, showing in every sweat-stained doublet and cartwheel ruff. It all made me feel frightfully sick.

At the last minute there had been what proved to be a rather unfortunate attempt to erect canopies over some of the stalls to protect the stall-holders, many of whom were in padded or fur-lined costumes, from the direct rays of the sun. An over-eager schoolboy-corsair, anxious to help, slipped on a bar above one of the cattle-pens and broke his leg and was carried away on a stretcher. Mrs Bethenna left early, having purchased a mere half-dozen poker-work "novelties" and a stencilled cushion cover, the paint on which was not yet completely dry; a Tudor merchant's wife fainted in the heat; and when, later on, the wooden plank supporting the canopy above the flower stall over which the doctor's wife and Miss Penfound were presiding fell and struck the latter on the shoulder, she too passed out. Borne from the scene by the doctor and the "nice, kind, sensible, steady woman", who had replaced Bethany at The Haven and driven home in the doctor's own car, she was later reported to be "badly shaken".

In September, a new term had started. I was very taken up with my new life and interests at the Art School, and that meant classes every day, including one on Saturday mornings, so that I was only at home on Sundays and I did not see Miss Penfound again for several weeks. But even I soon became aware that there was "something going on" locally; something covert, scandalous, not to be referred to directly or discussed openly but very much there nevertheless, and obviously common knowledge.

Outside the church porch there was a low brick wall on which some of the Sunday School children occasionally scribbled remarks along "Willie loves Winnie" lines, adorned with drawings of hearts pierced with arrows. Though rather silly, they were considered so harmless that they were usually allowed to remain until obliterated by time and the weather. But recently writing of a very different nature had been appearing on the walls of the porch itself; writing which, when erased, was persistently renewed. Presumably of a salacious nature, it concerned a supposed relationship not between the Willies and Winnies of the parish but (of all people) Miss Penfound and Dr Challis. There was not of course the slightest evidence for this unprecedented suggestion. Dr Challis, who had been called to The Haven about a week after the Fayre, had afterwards assured the sensible domestic that there was nothing to worry about. Miss Penfound's shoulder was quite healed, and as her present malaise was due solely to her having reached a "difficult age" it would be unnecessary for him to call again. As far as was known, he and Miss Penfound had not met since.

Probably most people did not believe it anyway. The good-looking doctor was well liked. So was she, and both of them were highly respected. But it was a serious allegation to make against anyone in his profession and if believed could lead to his being struck off the medical register. For her it was almost worse, coming as it did on top of the Bethany affair, though naturally neither showed any outward emotion, facing it out on Sunday mornings in church with characteristic panache, knowing every eye was upon them, neither either speaking to or, it was carefully noted, even looking at one another.

The culprit (or culprits) always used red chalk and appeared to work in the early hours of the morning or even during the night, as the inscriptions were always first seen by early arrivals for the eight o'clock communion service.

One of the sidesmen who was a retired army sergeant volunteered to sleep in the church and keep a twenty-four-hour watch, armed with a horsewhip. "And if I ever catch these filthy young devils —" His offer was declined, and instead the verger arranged to come early himself. Although none of the younger people was directly suspect, the graffiti apparently being of a rather sophisticated nature, several choir boys were seized and searched for coloured chalks, but their pockets yielded nothing more incriminating than chewing gum. "It was," said the vicar, "the product of diseased imaginations," when at last referring publicly to "the recent defacement of the church porch," one night after evensong.

I myself had never seen these inscriptions or drawings or whatever they were. My mother, who rarely went to bed before midnight, was not an early riser and so we were never among the first of the congregation to arrive, usually slipping in at the last minute, just as the service was about to begin. Then one morning I went alone. My mother and sister were still asleep when I let myself out of the front door at exactly twenty minutes to eight by the dining-room clock. It was a pleasant walk through the autumn morning, past familiar vistas softened by the early light. Vapour rising from the river lay in little hollows in the hills; and higher up the ground, gilded by the level rays of the sun, was lighter than the sky. It was also exceptionally quiet for that time of the morning. As I walked up the church path it occurred to me that, not having heard the ten-to-eight train leave the station and having met no one on the way, I was in fact not very early but very late and the service would be already well under way. Then quite suddenly I realised what had happened. It was of course the end of "Summer Time" that weekend and all the clocks would have been put back an hour at midnight; that is, all but ours. And so instead of being eight o'clock it was actually not yet seven.

The pathway ran parallel with and close to the south wall of the church so that anyone approaching along it was invisible to anyone standing in the porch (and vice versa) until they were practically face to face. So it was not until I actually reached the porch that I saw that someone was there before me. Miss Penfound was standing with her back towards me, bending forward and vigorously scraping the wall with what I assumed was a duster or wiping cloth of some sort, evidently attempting to erase what was evidently written there. There was a holy water stoup in the wall and it was around the stone work surrounding this little niche that what at first looked like additional decoration, following the line of the carving, had been added in red chalk. So this was it.

Here were no hearts pierced by love's arrows, but instead several other organs of the human body inscribed with the names of the two persons concerned, depicted with startling realism.

She must have heard me coming and turned and dropped what was in her hand. For a moment I thought she must imagine that the drawings were mine, and that having been lurking in the churchyard I had now returned to witness her distress, for I could think of nothing else to account for her look of utter rage. What she had been holding when I came in now lay on the flagstones between us, and as I stooped to pick it up and return it to her she brushed angrily past me through the doorway. She ran along the path towards the gate, and as she ran she was also weeping.

She left the town a few days later and The Haven was put up for sale the following week, after the furniture had been moved out by men who came with a long distance removal van which then departed for an unknown destination. Locally it was assumed that, greatly distressed by the recent scandal concerning herself, she had simply and very understandably fled, poor thing. The fact that she never wrote to anyone in the town seemed to fit in with this explanation. And of course she never knew that I never spoke of what I had seen, and never did till now. For what Canon Penfound's daughter held in her hand on that morning long ago was not a duster or an eraser of any kind but a stick of red chalk.

CHAPTER TEN

The Greenstone Promontory

The time came when I passed City and Guilds exams in Embroidery and Design — one of the youngest ever to achieve the top grade — and gained my Art Teaching Certificate. Once, later, when a fit of pique and despondency at my seeming lack of prospects came over me for a moment, I made the dramatic gesture of throwing my hard-worked-for, hard-won Art School qualifications, along with some other for the moment scorned and despised personal possessions, down an old mine shaft. That mood and gesture were, fortunately, short-lived.

Soon afterwards, to my great sadness and sorrow, we decided to leave Cornwall, at least for the time being, for a trial spell in the London area, where perhaps my work prospects might be better, but also for the other usual haunting or hunted reasons.

I shall never forget our last glimpses of the great cliffs and tumbling tides of Cornwall and, as we made our farewell crossing of the Tamar Estuary, of all the beloved familiar landscapes and landmarks where magic had so much — so well nigh ever — been in my eyes.

From time to time I was bound to go back to "Lyonesse", whether for long or short stays, when it was always a sort of home-coming, but I was never again to live there.

I managed to find more or less congenial work after we had settled for a while in a still somewhat rural Ruislip. Though by then included in outer London, it had (if I remember rightly) its own Metropolitan District railway station at a point where the Underground had become overground. Perhaps less congenial in some ways, for the hours in the basement were long and arduous, yet not entirely without solace, was a spell of working in the "Needlewoman" embroidery studios in Regent Street. Between there and Ruislip I travelled to and fro every day, sometimes staying on for an evening at the theatre, which was one of my compensations, or to be taken out to dinner by a kindly canon. More completely congenial work was the writing and illustrating of technical articles on needlecraft for *The Teachers' World* and some other stitchwork periodicals, for which I was soon remuneratively commissioned. Most triumphant and promising of all would have been my specially commissioned series of original embroidery designs in colour, scheduled to appear in two books to be produced by the well-known French firm of Dolfus-Mieg, based in Paris. But it came too near to the eve of war, and was never finally consummated — though I did get paid for the designs. All this is merely what kept me in London — following what proved to have been a momentous visit to Cornwall.

As a child in West Cornwall during the 1920s I was always expecting something to happen, some momentous, vaguely supernatural event after which the whole world would be changed; or if not exactly changed, at least for ever seen anew. It is odd that when, twenty years later, something of this kind did occur I did not, at the time, think it strange nor realise its nature until long after. In fact, the day of days when it finally came was very much like those which had preceded it. But during childhood I lived at times in almost hourly anticipation, and there were certain spots where, more than at others, the possibility appeared likely: where rumour of some great event seemed borne upon the very pulses of the air.

At Angarrack, a village about two miles from where we lived in Hayle, there was a narrow lane no wider than a footpath but with high leafy hedges, where in spring the first violets were always to be found, and which twisted up the hillside, not zigzagging but turning for ever in the same direction like a spiral. The narrowness of the path and density of the hedges made me feel that, enchanted and ensnared, I trod a maze. I never knew where it led for I never reached the end, which I longed to see, though I rather feared to find.

Then there were the sand-dunes and the shore, stretching from the sand-bar and quicksands of Hayle estuary to the mouth of the Red River at Gwithian three miles away. The dunes, a shifting boundary between land and sea, were a breeding ground for fantasy at all times. For there were stories of an oratory, farms, and even a whole village, disappearing overnight in the blown sand.

Inland were outworked tin and copper mines in the hills beyond the town. Of these Wheal Alfred was the largest, giving its name to a whole district that included a farm and several cottages as well as the old workings. There were always pretty stones to be found among the mine-waste, and occasionally a small piece of silver as well. But the most fascinating thing about the area, the thing which made it more interesting and infinitely more dangerous than even the quicksands, was a deep, wide, wholly unprotected shaft. Here, where earth yawned, flowers grew in the very mouth of the abyss. Fair-days (silverweed) and brimble roses bloomed as far as one could see down into the darkness.

Originally my great event was conceived in terms of finding hidden treasure, very understandably, as this theme was central to so many fairy tales. And then for one whole summer it centred around the figure of an ancient Cornish King, whose palace had been buried in the sand over a thousand years ago, and whom I hoped to see. Given a King, treasure and other splendours would naturally follow. Meanwhile, as no one knew where he was actually buried, any flower of the dunes might have sprung from his tomb; the trumpets of viper's bugloss, the solitary sunflower hanging like a sacred monstrance in the air might have been nourished by the princely dust. I was sure he would come, not all at once, but gradually. After all, if the little spring flowers could rise so certainly from the dead under-growth and winter's mud of the mazy path, why should

212

not one day his royal purple dye the ground and from among the glistening spears of sea-holly his eyes look out?

As time passed my expectation grew if anything stronger, more like a certainty. But the overall conception altered and I no longer thought of treasure and kings. Gradually the idea of "finding" changed to "seeing", and finally to the thought of a Sight which would also be a Knowing, like an answer. I had heard of a burning question and so, inevitably, there must also somewhere be a burning answer.

I was ten years old when we left Hayle and I did not see that part of the country again until a brief stay in Penzance with an American friend during 1937. Merle was interested in geology and every day we tirelessly traversed the coastal paths and what she always referred to as "the granite moors" in search of each and every one of the carefully listed sites she had travelled so far to find.

On the last day of our stay we went to Cape Cornwall, "the greenstone promontory and the only Cape in England", which was about a mile from the mining village of St Just and which, determined as usual to miss nothing, she insisted that we must view. Greenstone was apparently an exceptionally hard granite, rather different from the grey Cornish granite of the Land's End area which we had spent the morning surveying. It was already quite late in the day when we got to St Just, and by the time we reached Cape Cornwall the bright sunshine had changed to a scattered light, obscuring the horizon. Skyline and sea so merged that in places far out, where an occasional ray of sun pierced the low cloud and fell on the sea below, it appeared as if the sky itself was laced with the bright water.

I had not been greatly in favour of this piece of extra sight-seeing when it had first been suggested, but looking back at the mainland from the Cape I was very glad that we had come. To the south the coast was visible as far as Land's End. But it was the northward view, to the left as I looked back from the mine-stack at the head of the promontory, that held my gaze. Here mine ruins like crusader castles stretched towards a headland about a quarter of a mile away. At its foot two engine houses had been built on the rocks and around them the sea, forced into a narrow vent below, rose in a torrent of foam and blown spray, drenching the ruins, the massive walls of which streamed with salt water.

It was quite different from Wheal Alfred, the only other mine I knew. It was like some ultimate reality and charged with a secret meaning. A place to come to at the last, to breathe one's last. Or to come to in sorrow, for the scene was stricken enough to out-match any human suffering. It was like looking at the wreck of the world. For a little while I watched the glassy sea (green and transparent near the shore, almost purple farther out) surge, swell and break with a curious sighing sound around the monstrous rocks. Both sight and sound were slightly hypnotic, so strange they seemed to cast a spell, and I would have liked to linger. But Merle, whose interest and enthusiasm had suddenly evaporated at the thought of having to climb the Cape, had remained

THE GREENSTONE PROMONTORY

behind at the foot of the path and was now waiting and impatiently signalling to me to come down.

Back in London in Trafalgar Square a few evenings later we were selling *Peace News*, the weekly paper published by the recently formed Peace Pledge Union, when we tangled with two "blackshirts", members of Mosley's British Union of Fascists, who were there to sell copies of their paper, *Action*. The fracas was purely verbal, but Merle and I were both wearing sandwich-boards bearing the Peace Pledge Union motto "War! We Say No!", in large letters. A small crowd started to gather and in my agitation and not being able to see where I was treading, I tripped on the edge of the pavement and fell. Merle, similarly encumbered, was unable to assist me but I was helped to my feet by a tall young man wearing a rather shabby raincoat and an old Etonian tie, who then proceeded to retrieve the papers I had dropped which, now scattered on the ground, were beginning to blow away.

In the Lyons Tea Shop where the three of us went later, Basil Harvey James told us something of himself and said that though he was a socialist he was not a pacifist and would join up immediately if there was a war. It had suddenly become the kind of day when one no longer thought of time and we must have talked for hours. It was eleven o'clock and they were clearing the tables before closing for the night when we rose to go. Then it was that he noticed a copy of *Coral Island* which Merle had bought in Charing Cross Road earlier in the day to send to her young brother in America. He told us that his family had owned the tin mine about which Ballantyne had written *Deep Down*, another of his boys' adventure stories, and which had appealed to him as a setting, being on rocky cliffs with galleries running out under the sea.

I said that there was a mine on the cliffs near St Just in Cornwall with engine houses on the rocks at the very edge of the sea. "Yes," he answered. "That is it. That is Botallack, my great-great-grandfather's mine."

From the moment when he had first appeared in the square, all during the evening while we were talking, and in the weeks that followed, he seemed like someone known long since.

We were married within the year.

We spent the Christmas of 1939 at Wheal Alfred Farm. It was the first Christmas of the war and Basil, who had joined up as he had always intended to, was on leave.

War had been declared four months earlier, in September, and everyone had expected bombs on London and hundreds dying in the streets within the first few hours, but nothing like that had happened. In fact, hostilities had not yet started and it seemed still just possible that they never would. Even the sad King's faltering broadcast, which we all listened to in the great kitchen at Wheal Alfred on Christmas Day, held out this wonderful hope for the New Year with the words, ". . . and if it should bring peace."

It was to be the last Christmas in the world as we had known it.

There was snow and a great frost which lasted for most of the time we were there. The days were very sunny and the snow mostly came at night; each day it would start around twilight with feathery flakes falling like flowers and every morning we looked out at an untrodden world which was lighter than the sky.

By the afternoon the sun would have partly thawed the ice, and in places thrown long shadows through the luminous mist. Occasionally an overloaded branch, relieved of its weight of snow, sent down a sparkling crystal shower and silver trees blazed with white fire instead of candles.

The solitude, the silence, the great landscape of light, all combined to make this curious season a timeless no-man's-land between peace and a war that might yet never be.

The farmer came from a family of Hayle tinners who had emigrated to the silver mountain region of Mexico when Wheal Alfred was abandoned during the depression of the 1860s but had later returned and bought the farm.

In the small room which he used as an office there were a number of books about Cornwall, mining journals and old copies of the *Emigrant and Colonial Gazette*. An engraving of Botallack hung over the fireplace. Entitled simply *Greenstone Rocks, Botallack*, it was a view of the headland and the engine houses on what I now knew were the Crown Rocks and was evidently drawn from the same spot as that from which I had seen it.

The books and papers contained a good deal of information about the mine, and it was the simple facts that pleased. One report by the Royal Geological Society of Cornwall listed a number of the minerals concentrated in and around the Crowns. "Purple copper ore, opal, amethyst, jasper and chalcedony, garnets both yellow and red . . . This mine was wrought beneath the sea beyond the memory of any man now living." It was like reading a prose poem.

Travellers described the seaward galleries as being "under the pathway of the great ships and the playground of the leviathan", the engine houses as "works worthy of Virgil's Vulcan and the smiths of Lipari." And there was an eloquent account by Wilkie Collins of a descent to the "sunless galleries . . . our path a strange one . . . flame burning on our heads and darkness enveloping our limbs . . . flaring our candles hither and thither to see the bright copper streak the dark and lustrous green traversed by red veins of iron." All of which I thought very fine and splendid until Basil dismissed them as grossly overwritten. As a socialist he was averse to the idea of private ownership in any form, especially ownership of the land, the source of all wealth.

Botallack had an ominous side. Exceptionally difficult to work, it was also in perpetual danger of flooding, both by the sea and from the already flooded sections, or "houses of water", as they were called. Accidents underground were frequent, with men trapped by falling rock. One of the mining journals contained an account of a thunderstorm in which lightning, having destroyed an engine house roof and chimney, glanced down the shaft and, flashing another three hundred fathoms, struck those working at the far end of it. A miner worked ten hours a day, and one of the harshest conditions of his employment was that he was paid only on the amount of copper and tin he actually raised so that, should he strike an area of rock without ore, he could go for weeks without earning anything.

Conscious of the load of suffering which he said must have been inflicted on human lives under such conditions, I think that Basil saw the history of the mines primarily as an account of extreme hardship and preventable disaster. For this reason he had never liked Ballantyne's *Deep Down: A Tale of the Cornish Mines*, with its implied indifference to what, in the author's day, were considered to be the lower classes. Basil had been especially shocked by the casual description of a man whose eyes had been destroyed by a prematurely detonated fuse "in the usual way." This blinded miner was long afterwards to be recalled by one of Cornwall's finest poets, D. M. Thomas. His knowledge of the underground labyrinth was such that "when the guttering candles failed" he became a guide to those with eyes: "one man guided them unfailingly through blackwaters. He was blind".

In Penzance one morning towards the end of our stay, the day being clear and bright, less like winter than spring, I said I would like to go to Botallack. Basil instantly agreed and suggested that on the way we could look at the church in St Just where there were several windows dedicated to the memory of members of his family, one of them including an unusual view of the sea and cliffs at Land's End, and none of which I had ever seen.

There was something about the interior of the church which struck me immediately on entering as being more like a natural formation than the work of man, an impression emphasised by the unusual appearance of the walls, which had been stripped of plaster, the natural stone being pointed with pitch lining and in places with undressed blocks of moorland granite.

On the North wall, where some of the plaster still remained, were two fifteenth-century wall paintings. One of them depicted St George and the Dragon. The other was an almost life-size figure of Christ in rust, dull red and chalky blue, surrounded by a collection of mining and agricultural tools of the period. The figure, young and clean-shaven and naked but for a loin cloth, one long end of which had come undone and hung by his side, was of powerful build, all but his hands which, small and tender, were raised to a wound in his breast from which blood streamed through his fingers and spattered the wall around. The realism of the blood-stained disarray was startling. It was a humanist conception, the embodiment of human toil and suffering, and of a different kind of being from the saints and archangels depicted elsewhere in the church around it.

There were a few local men in the pub where we presently went for a drink. All had been miners when they were young and now they were old, all but one, a fine-looking man slightly younger than the rest, with very blue eyes and a glance like summer lightning, who, from the crutches lying on the stone floor beside him, appeared to be a cripple. Visitors were few and far between and two strangers were obviously of great interest, especially when one of them wore battle-dress. They seemed genuinely pleased to see us, at once made room for us on a bench by the fire, and wanted to know all about us. How long had we been married . . . any little ones . . . and what had brought us there that morning?

In reply to our own questions about the church that we said we had come to see, they seemed to know nothing of the origin of the mysterious Christ of the Trades painting, though the lame miner who was sitting next to us, who, with his air of wounded strength might almost have served as a model for the figure, said that it would have had some connection with Christ having come to Cornwall as a young man with his uncle, Joseph of Arimathea, who was himself a tinner — and the others agreed. They said that Joseph, searching for metal, had come to Ding Dong, the mine beyond Levant, which was itself beyond Botallack; and the soft ring of their voices sounding the wonderful names was like the sound of bells tolling underground. It was interesting that, down-to-earth "hard-rock" men as they were, they spoke of this coming as fact and not legend. It was really very much as they spoke of the coming of John Wesley less than two hundred years ago.

Later, when it was time for us to go, Basil went up to the bar with the empty glasses and I was about to follow him when the lame man who had spoken of Joseph of Arimathea stopped me.

"Where to now 'en, my love?" he asked, his fine, good face full of kindness. And on hearing that we were on our way to the mine, "Ah Botallack," he said sadly. "'Tis a berrin' ground. Our dear ones lie there. 'Tis a tomb."

There was a terrible finality about the words. And it was as though the day suddenly grew dark. At that moment Basil, who had been over to the door, returned to say that as a heavy sea-mist had come up and there was now no possibility of going on we should catch the bus, which had just driven up and was waiting in the square, to go back to Penzance.

Early in April Basil, having completed his army training, was posted to France and in June he was reported "missing." Stunning as this news was, there was a likelihood that a British soldier reported as missing after the fall of France had either been taken prisoner or had escaped into the surrounding countryside and was being sheltered there, especially one who spoke French like a Frenchman as Basil did, and so might hope to escape detection by the Germans. The months went by, and the longer the silence continued the more probable it seemed that he was still alive.

The following spring I went to stay with my mother at the cottage she had rented near Hayle, which meant that I was able to revisit some of my childhood haunts. I often went down to the sea, where the sky above the bay appeared much higher than I ever remembered seeing it, and bluer: an infinity, almost a blaze of blue. On a sunny day the empyrean was also the region of fire, and one could almost imagine that something not yet visible beyond the horizon glanced in the upper air and added its lustre to the sky. With the return of the light and the violets around the mazy path came a wonderful upsurge of hope. Then, quite suddenly, it ended one morning with confirmation of Basil's death the previous summer.

A few days later I went up to St Just with the intention of walking over to the mine. The thought of going where we had once planned to go together brought an unexpected comfort. As I had never been there before and all sign-posts had been taken down because of the threat of invasion, I took a map which I soon realised I could not read. Or at least for some reason was unable to read correctly, as the place names on it appeared to be at total variance with the position of the actual places as I knew them in reality. Feeling completely mystified, I decided to go straight to Cape Cornwall from St Just, because from there I would know the way, as I clearly remembered seeing a wide track through the mine waste leading down to the engine houses on the rocks.

It was a strange walk from the village to the Cape, more like nearing the end of a long journey than an ordinary walk, and it felt as though a great deal of time was passing; so much, that by the time I got there I would have grown old. How the road wound, and how the mind wandered, fastening on any little thing for consolation! Somewhere I remembered having read that in the very heart of the great mine, whose flood waters were always briny or crimson from the mineral waste, like blood and tears, there was a little spring of fresh water at which the miners used to fill their flasks. I liked to think of that now. And then there were the men who had been struck by lightning in the depths and had not been killed nor even badly injured, only struck down, but had risen again and must have thought it was the

Resurrection, living to tell the tale, and very likely being listened to like those risen from the dead The gentle miner had called it a "berrin' ground". But was not the whole earth with its great load of flowers and graves our berrin' ground?

I met no one on the road and the solitude and violet light of afternoon perfectly accorded with my mood and wandering thoughts.

Long before I saw it I heard the sighing murmur of the sea, like a sound in my own head. When the promontory finally came in sight I had an irrational fear that I might yet never reach it and so began to hurry, almost to run towards it, as towards safety. Having reached it and, I thought, the longed for sight, the absence of that sight was for some moments like gazing on a thunderous void. For neither ruins nor track nor great rocks were to be seen. Instead, the northward view was bounded by a headland which I knew, from having seen pictures of it, to be Kenidjack, and slowly I realised that Botallack was on the far side and completely hidden. And strange as this moment was, this day and hour, I supposed they were as nothing compared with the mystery of that other day, four years earlier, when from the self-same spot I had seen Botallack and not seen High Kenidjack.

About an hour later, having used the map to follow the windings of the cliff path and bridle tracks, I at last came within sight of Botallack mine and the Crown Rocks, a scene already known by heart and which I now found in every aspect as I remembered it.

Postscript

One radiantly sunny day in May, during the war, I was going to pay a visit at the Whiteway Colony in the Gloucestershire countryside, on an afternoon off from my work as cook-house keeper for a conscientious objectors' land-working group. On the way I was to have been met by a pacifist acquaintance, but due to a misreading of his postcard I had come on the wrong day. As I stood waiting in that country lane by a bus-stop, not quite knowing what to do next or where to go, a bus drew up and a man got off it.

He looked straight at me as I stood there, and then asked me, "Are you looking for or waiting for somebody, or wanting to find the way somewhere?"

I soon explained.

"I am going to Whiteway, too," he said, "to have tea with Nellie Shaw. As your mistaken date has obviously left you stranded, why not come along to Nellie's with me? She won't mind an extra one."

Exchanging names then, I recognised him; Dion Byngham. "But I've just read an article of yours in *New Vision*," I told him delightedly.

After that tea with Nellie, one of the founders of the colony, Dion and I walked back through woods aglow with golden kingcups. So that was how it began.

Years later, on the anniversary of that meeting, Dion wrote me a sonnet about it:

By a green roadside still I see you stand
That timeless moment in the month of May;
To one fair face has changed the sunlit day,
In one small figure merged the meadowed land.

As by the tremor of a dowser's wand
We sense beneath what transient words we say
A spring that drinks the arid past away,
Soft rippling as I touch you, hand on hand . . .

Since when nine times has budding hawthorn been
Along with lilac plumed in fragrant greeting,
While blackbirds piped from bluebell scented green
Of nesting trees to celebrate our meeting:

And still all treasures seen or heard unite
In one dear voice, one face whence flowers the light.

I could not have asked for better than that.

*Note to pp. 178 & 181

The fraught relationships of the Flawes family are made explicable by the knowledge that Mabel was Erma's mother. It appears that Erma believed the deception that she was her sister all her life.

ISIS publish a wide range of books in large print, from fiction to biography. A full list of titles is available free of charge from the address below. Alternatively, contact your local library for details of their collection of ISIS large print books.

Details of ISIS complete and unabridged audio books are also available.

Any suggestions for books you would like to see in large print or audio are always welcome.

7 Centremead
Osney Mead
Oxford OX2 0ES
(01865) 250333